PROTOTYPING
AND MODELMAKING
FOR PRODUCT DESIGN
BJARKI HALLGRIMSSON

Laurence King Publishing

Published in 2012 by
Laurence King Publishing Ltd
361–373 City Road
London EC1V 1LR
Tel: +44 20 7841 6900
Fax: +44 20 7841 6910
email: enquiries@laurenceking.com
www.laurenceking.com

Reprinted 2013

Related study material is available on the
Laurence King website at www.laurenceking.com

CONTENTS

IMPORTANT NOTICE ON SAFETY

Chapter 5 of this book covers good health and safety practice, and a further series of safety checks have been included at the beginnings of Chapters 6 to 20 which cover tools, materials and processes. Chapter 8 features an overview of typical modelmaking tools and machines, but this chapter does not provide specific instruction on tool-operation, as it is beyond the scope of this book. The methods, processes, case studies and tutorials in this book are general in nature and should never be attempted without proper consultation, training and supervision from a professional shop technician. Although Laurence King Publishing and the author have taken steps to ensure the safety information provided is accurate and up-to-date at the time of writing, this information is not exhaustive, and they cannot assume responsibility for any improper use, changes, errors or omissions. The reader should be aware that he or she is responsible for his or her own safety and, potentially, that of any nearby individuals when undertaking the types of activities described herein and should govern himself or herself accordingly.

INTRODUCTION
Why We Prototype

Behind every successful product design is a story of numerous refinements and much hard work. The fact is that the transformation of an idea into a real product takes a great deal of work, involving more than simply creating pictures on the computer. Product design is a complex activity, which involves working with other people and disciplines, coming up with creative and useful ideas (that hopefully are also sustainable) and slugging through all the iterations of making something work and look good at the same time. One method that has always been used by designers, and continues to be embraced, is that of physical prototyping. The primary message of this book is that building and testing in 3D is a continuing and critical component of a successful design process. Whereas 3D Computer Aided Design (CAD) has made it easier to visualize, analyze and implement product solutions, physical prototypes can still be played with and scrutinized in a way that is not possible on screen. As a result they precede and complement most of the computer rendering and animations that happen in real-life projects. Just as the computer helps integrate interdisciplinary activities on screen, physical prototypes draw people together in face-to-face discussions that lead to a different level of interaction between clients, designers and end users.

Definition of Prototyping and Modelmaking

The terms *physical prototype* and *model* can be used interchangeably to describe a preliminary three-dimensional representation of a product, service or system. In recent years the use of the word 'prototype' has become favoured as it is more encompassing. A wide range of physical prototypes is used throughout the design process to simulate different aspects of a product's appearance and function before it is produced. This book will show why physical prototypes are essential to the design process, and how they are used to solve a range of problems associated with new product development. Each new version of a prototype or model is known as an iteration.

The Fiskars Multi-Snip pruning tool went through many iterations and evolutions, as shown in this progression of prototypes.

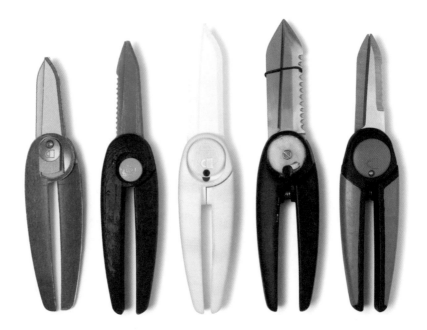

Prototyping and *modelmaking*, although inherently related terms, actually refer to different activities. Prototyping is a design method that uses physical prototypes to study and test how a new product will be used, and how it will look and be manufactured. Modelmaking, on the other hand, is the step-by-step method of producing the prototype. For this reason, this book has been divided into two sections: Prototyping and Modelmaking. The first section, Prototyping, describes what physical prototypes are and how they are used in product design and development. The second section, Modelmaking, specifically addresses the many issues regarding materials and options for construction. By being mindful of the reasons why we prototype, we should be able to make better choices about how we make prototypes.

A student examines progress on a drill appearance prototype in the lab.

Prototyping Is a Form of Problem Solving

Prototyping is a key problem-solving activity in product design. It starts right from the beginning of a project and continues right into production. Given the complexity of product development, it is critical to take as much of the guesswork out of the design process as possible, and prevent surprises from showing up later in a project. It is much less expensive to solve problems early in a project than later, when tooling may have been started and sales commitments made. Prototypes evolve along with the design process; simple prototypes serve as initial three-dimensional sketches and are then replaced by iterations of successively more refined versions.

The more complicated the product, the more disciplines will be involved and the more prototypes typically needed. Physical prototypes enable teamwork and collaboration, since they serve to gather team members around for discussion and reflection. The prototypes oblige the team to deal with real issues, which are more easily ignored in memos and verbal discussions alone. Prototypes are also used to study and compare alternative approaches. This includes testing everything from technical requirements of construction to usability.

Modelmaking

The rich design tradition of developing sensitivity to materials, manufacturing and workmanship is based on the idea of learning by doing, which goes back to the beginning of product design. We actually learn different things from making the prototype (modelmaking) than we do from using the prototype (prototyping). Material properties do not have any real connection to the world we live in unless we first inform our senses in a hands-on way. By experiencing real materials and processes, the material qualities gain meaning. The sensibility and experience attained from this process form the basis for intuition and are therefore essential for conceptualization.

Physical and Digital Prototypes

Product designers need to have competency in several skills, including sketching, CAD and modelmaking. These are all critical tools and should be used effectively and not exclusively. A workflow that shifts back and forth between different skills expands the creative possibilities and is more balanced.

Computer technology has completely changed the way in which products are conceived and developed. Virtual computer models allow us to visualize the product, see how parts fit together, calculate the weight and carry out performance simulations along the way. Physical prototypes, on the other hand, answer questions that are hard or impossible to address on the computer alone. These questions usually have to do with the qualitative human aspects. Whereas computer simulation can be used to verify many technical requirements, physical prototypes can be placed into real environments and have tangible qualities, such as weight, size and texture, that can be experienced at first hand. Experienced designers build a great many physical prototypes along with virtual computer models. It is not a question of physical versus digital, but rather a matter of how the two approaches complement each other best. The tutorials in this book show workflow that involves sketching, CAD and physical modelmaking used in a complementary fashion.

Building by Hand and Using Computers

All physical prototypes used to be built manually by hand. Nowadays, as will be shown later in this book, new digital technologies enable 3D computer files to be output to automated computer-controlled prototyping machines. This may create the impression that prototypes no longer need to be made by hand at all, but that would be far from the truth. As will be shown in the case studies in this book, early ideas are actually explored faster by hand. What starts as sketches and quick handmade models gradually migrates to the computer and eventually from there to rapid prototyping or CNC machining.

Chapter 7 discusses how manual and digital ways of working complement each other and how new technologies such as laser scanning help designers reverse-engineer handmade models into CAD. There is, in other words, a convergence happening between traditional hand skills and computer skills. The computer mouse is probably going to be increasingly displaced by more natural and fluid input devices, which electronically simulate the sketching and sculpture-making process. This has already happened with the digital sketching pad, where the stylus is now the input device. Similarly, 3D haptic devices allow for hand-forming digital models in space. Modern design process is evolving, requiring designers to have one foot inside and one outside the virtual world every step of the way.

The Fiskars post-digging tool was first made by hand and tested (left) before creating a 3D computer model in CAD (right).

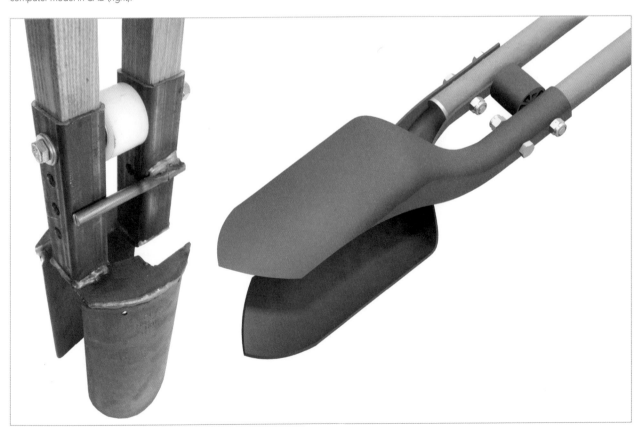

New interfaces are changing the way designers work. Products such as the Cintiq® interactive pen display (left) and the PHANTOM® haptic (force-feedback) device (below) blur the lines between analogue and digital methods of working.

Organization of this Book

The first chapters of the book explain why prototyping is so important to the design process. The many uses of prototyping will ultimately be shown in the context of several comprehensive projects by some of the world's leading design firms.

The second part of the book is an introduction to the typical materials used by designers in their prototyping efforts and how to work with them. In all cases the approach is to use digital and manual tools in a complementary and effective fashion. Tutorials were specifically developed for the book that underline the back and forth of digital and manual ways of working. The emphasis is on the kinds of construction that can be done by the designers themselves. Health and safety is stressed in terms of personal responsibility and awareness. As students leave their universities, they are likely not to have access to some of the world-class facilities to which they may have become accustomed. Being able to create models in simple materials in a healthy and safe manner will be important.

PROTOTYPING

CHARACTERISTICS OF PROTOTYPING

Successful prototyping requires thinking about building and making in a way that is different from the way we think about manufacturing and fabrication. First and foremost a prototype is not a final product. Before going into detail about how prototypes are used and before getting into the specifics of working with materials, it is worthwhile discussing some of the important characteristics of prototyping.

The Difference between Prototyping and Manufacturing

Prototyping and manufacturing are separate activities. Mass-manufactured products achieve their economy of scale through tooling. The time involved and the cost of making various types of tooling and setting up an assembly line, is a huge capital investment. Products have to sell in the thousands before this investment starts to pay off. Prototypes serve many purposes in order to reduce the risk associated with that level of investment. Since prototypes are built only in small numbers, they do not typically require any tooling and can be produced in a completely different fashion. At the early stages of a project, the focus may not even be on manufacturing at all, but on figuring out basic configurations and how the product will be used. As the design gets closer to production, it will be necessary to prototype all parts before tooling is made.

Material Substitution

Early on in a project, it is typically more cost- and time-efficient to substitute softer materials in place of production materials. Polyurethane foam, for example, is frequently sculpted to study the shapes of injection-moulded plastic parts, while a sheet of plastic can be painted in metallic pigment to look like sheet metal.

Functional configurations can also be simulated very quickly with simple prototypes. This is really useful when designing products that have internal components, as it allows the engineers and designers to play around with component placement in an effective and dynamic way.

A simple foamboard mock-up allowed engineers and designers to study internal component placement for the Motion Computing J3400 computer.

The Gyrus ENT surgical tool was developed by IDEO. The simple model on the left was quickly fashioned out of found materials during a meeting that paved the direction for the final design shown on the right. This shows the importance of trying things out early, even in simple found materials.

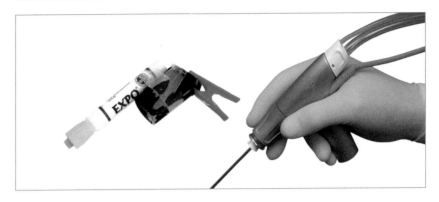

Iteration

The iterative aspect of prototyping is key. It is simply impossible and foolish to try to get everything right the first time. At one of the world's leading design firms, IDEO, the phrase 'fail often to succeed sooner' is used to describe how 'failure is the flip side of risk taking' (Kelley 2001). By discovering a failure in a prototype, something useful is learnt. That is critical to making sure that the product will work as intended. Being afraid of failure is really nothing more than taking unnecessary risk. The important thing is to subject the prototypes to enough evaluation and testing to expose possible failures beforehand. The sooner these problems are discovered the easier it is to accommodate changes to the design. Simple prototypes will expose obvious problems or show that an idea is viable. Every project has time and money constraints. These dictate the quantity of prototypes and iterations to be made. Physical prototyping does not have to be expensive, and, unlike computer simulations, can be used to get real information from real end users. Iteration is a major benefit of prototyping as many alternatives can be studied and compared.

Fidelity

The *Oxford English Dictionary* defines fidelity as 'the degree of exactness with which something is copied or reproduced'. Some materials, such as foamboard or polystyrene foam, are inherently low fidelity, as it is hard to get a lot of detail out of these soft materials. They are, however, easy and fast to work with. A high-fidelity model would be more exact and would typically have to be made in a harder material, which also takes longer to work with.

The idea of iterative product development involves solving big picture problems first, as opposed to fine details. Issues such as overall shape and size can therefore be studied first in low-fidelity materials, allowing for more speed and iteration. Examining the many iterations of the Oral-B toothbrush below, it is

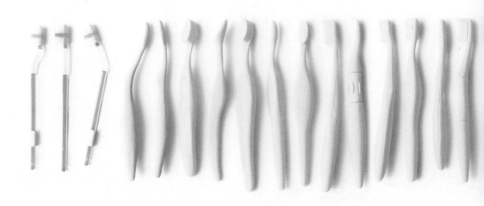

obvious how the early prototypes looked at options for the overall shape, whereas the later models made in harder, more exact materials included colouring and textural detailing. This is precisely why prototyping is both iterative and progresses from low to high fidelity.

Workmanship, Audience and Venue

The question of workmanship is a function of both skill and time invested. Fidelity should not be confused with level of workmanship. Modelmaking can still be careful and clean even when working at low fidelity. This is often a matter of audience. If the modelmaking is supporting a very quick and dirty prototyping effort that is done in order to study options as effectively as possible, then workmanship is not that important. When presenting the outcome of this exploration to an audience that is not well versed in design process, it does, however, become more important. In that case the level of detail may still be low, but the model will need to be more carefully constructed so as to convey the proper professionalism.

Looks-Like and Works-Like Prototypes

Design students may find that as they start working on complex products and experiences, they quickly become overwhelmed. At that point, prototyping may seem daunting, as there are so many things to test and understand. The case studies and examples in this book are meant to help illustrate how to break these larger problems into smaller, more focused prototyping exercises at the right level of fidelity. This is also a function of identifying the context: who is using the product, where and how?

Understanding how people interact with products is critical to framing the design and hence prototyping objective. Technological issues and human interaction aspects have to be looked at separately to some extent. This is because the human-use issues can become extremely clouded by technical assumptions and parameters, which in turn can limit any real innovation. When building prototypes it is therefore useful to distinguish between *looks-like* and *works-like* prototypes. The material qualities needed to explore form versus function are also different. A hard material may be needed for strength in the works-like prototype, whereas a softer material lends itself better to the sculptural complexity of the looks-like prototype. It is often much faster to build separate prototypes for this reason, and any necessary changes will be easier to implement.

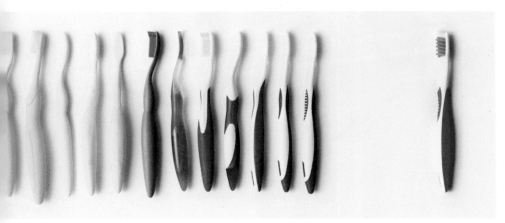

In the development of the Oral-B CrossAction® Toothbrush, Lunar Design, Palo Alto, made many models of body shapes as part of the iterative prototyping process.

Case Study Folding Hairdryer

This hairdryer project, by Wataru Watanabe (Carleton University, Ottawa) illustrates how prototyping progresses from low to high fidelity. It also illustrates the importance of getting the idea right before spending too much time on fine-tuning appearance. The idea behind this product is quite simple. It is to include a concentrator in a folding travel hairdryer. The design problem was that a concentrator, although a valuable feature for many users, adds extra bulk to an otherwise compact product.

During conceptualization, sketching was complemented by simple low-fidelity prototypes in paper and polystyrene foam. This showed that the concentrator could be fitted over a hairdryer handle with a wrapped-up cord. The low fidelity was appropriate as the focus was on the exploration of ideas. The pictures show how configuration issues such as overall size and storage compare to a more standard folding hairdryer.

The next step was to observe other people to see if they would find it easy and convenient to use the product as intended. This would necessitate a more robust low-fidelity prototype to allow people to perform the required tasks without breaking the prototype. A simple script was presented to participants (classmates in this case) and they were then photographed and interviewed to see what they thought. The outcome was important in deciding that in this case the handle should be thinner than competing models because that made it easier to roll up and fit the cord under the concentrator.

Once the design parameters were better understood it was time to start focusing on the appearance and detailed shape. Eventually the design progressed toward the final high-fidelity prototype.

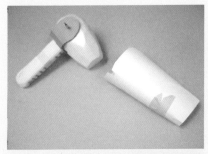

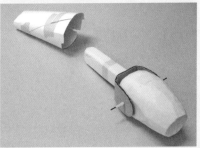

Foam and paper are used to explore the idea of a folding hairdryer with a concentrator. The prototypes show how the concentrator is stored on top of the handle.

A more robust wooden prototype was used to test the new configuration with end users. At the same time polystyrene foam models were made to study form (above)

With the configuration well tested, it is time to refine and finalize the design, again starting with low-fidelity materials, and progressing into a final detailed high-fidelity prototype.

Case Study Candela Luau

The Candela Luau™ is a sophisticated LED lantern designed with many uses in mind.

When designers Stefane Barbeau and Duane Smith of Vessel created the Luau™ portable LED lantern for OXO, they wanted to create a portable lighting product that could be used both inside and outside the house.

Some of the key features for the Luau™ were explored and confirmed through simple early prototypes that could be used to act out the scenarios that were important to the success of the product. A very simple works-like prototype was used to examine the idea of incorporating a dimmer into the bottom of the lantern, so that it could be dimmed by simply twisting it on the ground or while holding it. Stefane Barbeau says, 'we wanted to investigate if we could use the form of the lamp itself as an interface in order to simplify the action'. The placement and shape of the handle therefore became very important.

Although such a simple model was useful in exploring the basic functionality, the lantern itself needed to be explored more formally. It had to have a suitable aesthetic for indoor as well as outdoor environments. The shape also had to be comfortable to carry and easy to place on a charging base. Establishing overall form and proportion was done with a low-fidelity handmade looks-like polystyrene foam model. This model could be carried and placed in the relevant environments for evaluation by the design team.

The learning that was gained through these simple prototypes allowed the design team to start designing the product in 3D CAD with a sense of confidence. Once the 3D CAD data existed, it made sense to produce a more detailed prototype through rapid prototyping means. The levels of refinement and attention to detail now converged toward detailed design decisions and implementation.

This works-like model was used to explore the idea of dimming the light by rotating it on its own foot. Batteries were taped on to get a feel for the weight.

The convex cylindrical shape of the main body evoked the right visual semantics for the product's many uses. In order to achieve the hollow convex shape, the product would need to be blow-moulded. This presented some production challenges and needed to be verified. By working closely with the offshore supplier, the tooling and the production process were eventually worked out. It is important to realize that if this had not been the case, another design approach or design would have had to have been pursued.

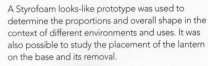

A Styrofoam looks-like prototype was used to determine the proportions and overall shape in the context of different environments and uses. It was also possible to study the placement of the lantern on the base and its removal.

The learning that was gained from the simple
models was an important first step before moving
ahead with 3D CAD. The cost and time invested in
3D CAD development and the rapid prototype
(foreground) were now more assured.

Sometimes a design presents manufacturing
challenges. In these cases, it is important to verify
that the shape can be made. Establishing that
the Luau™ lantern body could be blow-moulded
required some manufacturing experimentation.

A discreet indicator on the charging base changes
from orange while charging to green when fully
charged. The lantern illuminates automatically
when lifted or during a power outage. Such subtle
features were important to the quality and spirit of
the design and required further detailed design
development.

Case Study Motion Computing J3400 Tablet

The development of an innovative clip-on keyboard for the Motion Computing J3400 tablet computer shows the importance of testing functional aspects on their own with works-like prototypes. Before Mixer Design Group started designing the keyboard appearance in detail, it was more important to figure out how it should be used and how it would work in principle. The keyboard had to be easy to attach, as well as mechanically robust. By videotaping users interacting with works-like prototypes, the design team at Mixer Design Group were able to analyze replays and discuss their findings. The prototypes evolved from initial sketches and explorative models to reveal more promising design directions. The works-like prototypes had to incorporate stronger materials, such as aluminium, in order to work smoothly and to allow the designers to evaluate robustness.

A

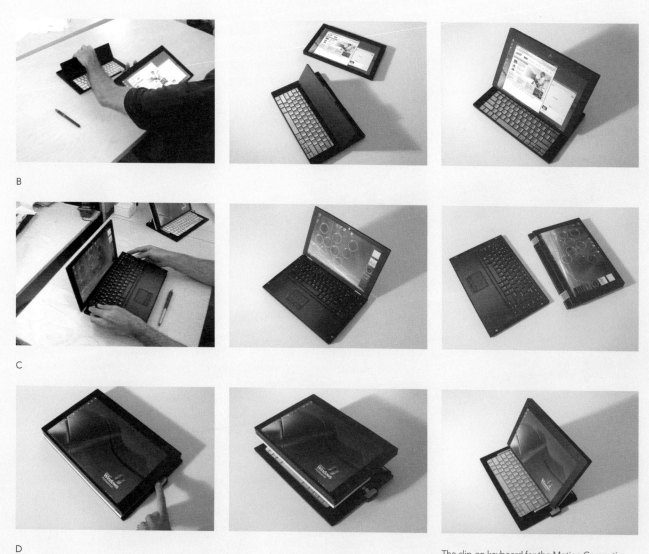

B

C

D

The clip-on keyboard for the Motion Computing J3400 tablet computer is a key aspect of the product's usability. Chosen options were developed further to investigate ease of use and convenience: (A) sliding keyboard model; (B) model incorporating the keyboard in the cover; (C) book-like mechanism; (D) four-bar linkage mechanism.

HOW PROTOTYPES ARE USED

Physical prototypes are used in myriad ways to solve problems and develop a better understanding of design requirements. In conjunction with sketches and other design methods they aid in: idea exploration, user testing, communication, design verification and standards testing. A single prototype often has more than one function: for example, exploration often involves some simple user testing as well. The following categorizations are not meant to be prescriptive, but rather draw attention to the many uses of prototypes.

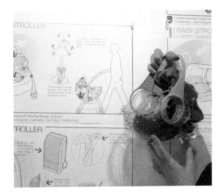
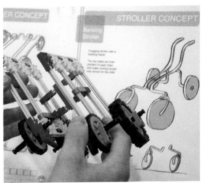
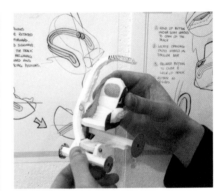

Carleton University students, to complement some of their early concepts for a new baby stroller design, used quick explorative prototypes. Kinex, foamboard and found objects were among some of the different approaches chosen by the students to help communicate the ideas.

Explorative Idea Generation

Just as brainstorming and sketching are fundamental to ideation, the physical dimension allows materials to be experienced in a hands-on, playful way that is not possible through two-dimensional visualization alone. Explorative prototyping involves rapid and sequential modelmaking to supplement sketches. This quickly helps to gauge whether an idea is worth pursuing and may even lead to fruitful unexpected insights, and hence to more innovative products. A low level of fidelity is often enough to serve as a proof of concept. Different organizations will have different names for explorative prototypes. The term breadboard or mock-up is often used to describe a low-fidelity works-like prototype, whereas low-fidelity looks-like prototypes are often called sketch or massing models. In this book the term 'explorative' is more encompassing as it describes any quickly made prototype for examining alternative emerging ideas. Functional exploration is usually highly experimental and rough. Sometimes products are taken apart and recombined into new functional creations. Mechanisms or other elements of the product may even be built in Lego® to get a feel for how it works, which in turn provides a foundation for the next iteration.

Exploration has everything to do with curiosity and discovery. Exploring new materials or technologies is just as important as exploring form and function. The famous Finnish architect Alvar Aalto developed his innovative laminated birchwood furniture through an extensive prototyping approach. This is even more important today, given new technologies and emphasis on sustainable design. For example, the Nike Trash Talk shoe evolved from designers at Nike exploring how to produce a quality athletic shoe using leftover materials so as to reduce its environmental impact.

The Nike Trash Talk shoe.

Exploration of form (sketch or massing models) usually starts in low-fidelity materials such as foamboard, cardboard or polystyrene foam. The approach is often to work directly from a quick sketch rather than to create exact drawings. Speed is of the essence in order to examine different options effectively before committing to a particular design direction.

Professional product designers build many early prototypes to generate and explore ideas in conjunction with sketching and computer work.

In the development of the ball-flinger dog toy, Mixer Design Group generated explorative models to visualize and evaluate ways in which to throw and pick up the ball. By building a set of early works like prototypes they were better able to evaluate different ideas and approaches quickly and effectively.

 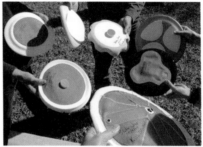 

An explorative prototyping approach informs the designers' thinking and often leads to unexpected insights gained from experimentation and testing. These insights in turn lead to more innovative products because the designers learnt something new that could be incorporated into the design.

Mixer Design Group developed the StarMark disc-shaped fetch toy for dogs through a process that involved a series of explorative prototypes in addition to sketching and computer work.

Guidelines for Exploration:

— These prototypes are mostly built for yourself, to help you understand what you are doing.
— Keep the model simple and free of details that detract from its purpose.
— Make appropriate use of materials. Also use materials to experiment.
— Build models in parallel to explore different issues, for example, works-like versus looks-like prototypes.
— Think of the prototype as disposable. This is an experiment to answer questions: try to learn from the model.

User Testing

A modern design approach involves ongoing research into how people interact with a new product, interface or service. Designers use prototypes to look at what people can and want to do, instead of making assumptions about their behaviour and preferences. By doing this early on in the design process, the observations form a framework for user-centred design requirements. This has become one of the most compelling and significant uses for physical prototypes because it is impossible to test the user experience of a physical product through the computer alone. Prototypes are thus used to test a range of ergonomic considerations, including human fit and size as well as cognitive issues.

The testing cycle consists of building a prototype, testing it with real end users and then observing the outcome of this interaction. This type of ethnographic research is greatly aided by prototypes and includes videotaping of participants to uncover obvious problems or to verify that the design is proceeding in the right direction. Testing can lead to some interesting and unexpected design opportunities. The more alternatives that are investigated, the more will be learnt.

The iterative test cycle includes observation of end users.

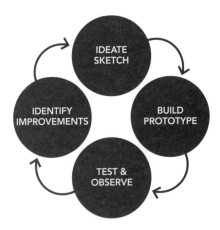

The starting point is often simple handmade prototypes in low-fidelity materials. Sometimes the entire environment of use may need to be prototyped, for example the interior of a car or aeroplane. By focusing on people and their interactions, the prototypes can be kept simpler in construction. This allows more options to be explored and changes to be made. Paper prototyping is a technique for testing a screen-based interface with a series of paper templates that mimic the software.

Simple low-fidelity prototypes in cardboard, in conjunction with paper prototypes of the screen interface, establish the interaction sequence and overall design requirements for this student project for a post-office kiosk.

The post-office kiosk was user-tested with a full-scale low-fidelity prototype (right). Once the product configuration and architecture had been completely tested, the final design detailing and manufacturing considerations had to be taken into account. The final design was communicated through a third-scale appearance prototype (far right).

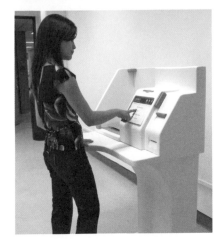

Full-scale prototypes help to finalize task flow and design requirements. The fidelity is gradually increased as more details are resolved.

Participants

Choosing the right participants is an important consideration. Whereas classmates might be useful for pilot studies, it becomes important to enlist the right end users in order to make the correct observations. This is also an opportunity to address a more inclusive design process by considering universal access issues in regards to people with disabilities. Suggested further reading is listed at the end of this book. Consider the rights of the people participating in your testing. If the information is to be published or shared, then privacy rules apply. Fortunately there are many good resources for conducting ethical studies, and universities require that all studies involving participants have ethics approval. Common sense obviously dictates that participants should never be involved in something that could have any adverse effect, especially regarding safety. User testing is only for the purpose of seeing if people can easily use the product: the prototypes are never to be used in testing strength or any other aspect that could potentially put the participants in harm's way.

Guidelines for Usability Testing:

— Be clear about the test and the tasks and build the model for that specific purpose.
— Obtain guidance on participant selection or refer to books on usability testing.
— Consider universality by including people with disabilities where necessary.
— Explore use from a general context into a more specific context. The overall experience and purpose is the starting point, as opposed to how the buttons should be arranged.
— Observe and document all interactions.
— Make sure to obtain ethics approval before testing with participants.
— Use electronic prototyping toolkits to prototype the experience.
— Never make prototypes that in any way expose the participant to any possible harm. If in doubt do not proceed and instead get expert help.

Communication

Product design is inherently an interdisciplinary activity. Product designers frequently need to communicate their ideas to end users, engineers and marketing professionals, who are not necessarily looking at the project from the same viewpoint. In the film industry, storyboards visually communicate design decisions such as the setting, costumes and story in a comic-book format. A series of still photographs with participants using physical prototypes and acting out intended scenarios can be used in the same way, to show other stakeholders how the product will be used and how it fits into its intended environment. This form of interdisciplinary communication is important in order to make sure that everyone involved with a new product's design and market release is consulted.

This student-built appearance prototype clearly communicates the design details and innovative tool-less maintenance features.

Appearance Prototypes

After idea exploration and testing with end users, the design of a product will progress toward a higher level of detail and refinement. High-fidelity looks-like prototypes are used to communicate the final appearance of the product. These final appearance models also have several prototyping uses, such as presentations to clients for sign-off before final tooling investment is made. They can also be displayed at trade shows, or used for professional product photography to announce a new product release.

This type of prototype is very much about visual refinement. Not only should the form and edges be precise and include exact edge radii, but manufacturing details such as parting lines and paint finishes should also be accurate down to the actual surface texture of the parts. Graphics will be applied to add final realism as well as to confirm placement. This level of detail can be created in computer renderings, but there is an aspect of reality that can only be appreciated through holding and turning something physical in one's hands for closer examination.

The level of skill and amount of time involved in making such models is very high. In professional practice they are almost exclusively built from 3D CAD files, either with high-resolution 3D rapid prototyping equipment or by Computer Numerical Control (CNC) machining of the parts. These processes are described in detail in Chapter 8: Tools (pages 65–78). CNC machining parts in high-density polyurethane foam has often been the preferred approach to making appearance models. This gives a high-resolution surface finish that requires very little finishing beyond painting. Increasingly, parts made by rapid prototyping are exhibiting the same surface quality and are used interchangeably.

The student project at top left demonstrates how an appearance prototype was used to communicate both the form and innovative features for a new electric chainsaw. The idea was to simplify regular electric chainsaw maintenance. The appearance prototype does not work, but it clearly communicates how this design simplifies chain lubrication and replacement. The oversized oil refill cap and chain release are both designed to release without tools, which is quite obvious by looking at the prominent visual cues in these interface areas.

Insight Product Development created appearance prototypes to communicate the final design intent of the redesigned Motorola NFL headsets and to make sure the Motorola brand would be visible on national television.

Physical Context of Use

Physical prototypes have the benefit of being able to be studied in their real physical context of use. Teams at Motorola Consumer Experience Design Group and Insight Product Development collaborated with the US National Football League (NFL) to redesign the NFL coaches' headsets. The final design included three different configurations that were prototyped as high-fidelity appearance models. The appearance models were instrumental in making sure that the Motorola brand was clearly visible on national television. This included the use of actual broadcast video to examine different logo options in snow and autumn outdoor lighting situations.

Guidelines for Building Prototypes for Communication:

— Who is the audience? Where will they see the prototype and when?
— What is being communicated? Will the prototype be on display or will it be used for a demonstration purpose?
— Is it something that should be done in-house or should it be sent to a professional modelmaker?
— Think about communicating corporate identity, colour options, textures and other details.
— A full-scale appearance model is an opportunity to examine the product in its intended environment of use.

Design Verification

Many aspects of a product have to be tested and optimized prior to mass production. Digital CAD simulation has become an essential part of the process to verify overlapping issues with regard to appearance, manufacturing and performance. Some common simulation features include assembly part interference checking to ensure that parts fit together properly, and photorealistic rendering to verify that the product will look as intended. More advanced tools include Finite Element Analysis to check for stresses, strains and deflection during static loading or drop testing. CAD models can in turn be output to 3D printed models (see rapid prototyping in Chapter 8). These can be fitted with working breadboards and other working components to create fully functional prototypes as shown in Chapter 3.

Verification Aspects	Physical Prototypes	Digital Simulation
Aesthetics and branding	Appearance model	CAD rendering
Task mapping	Working prototype	3D animation
Manufacturing fit	3D printed parts	Part interference checking
Mechanisms	3D printed parts	Kinematic analysis
Strength	Machined components	Finite element analysis
Heat dissipation	Working prototype in lab	Heat transfer analysis

The table above shows how digital and physical prototyping complement each other. There are distinct advantages to both. Virtual simulation can happen very quickly and is useful to study the effects of loading and other functional parameters.

At the same time it is impossible to verify ergonomic issues such as comfort without real physical prototypes. In the NFL coaches headset redesign (page 24), it was necessary to verify the comfort and wearability of each one of the three distinct and different headsets through physical prototypes that could be worn and tested.

Technical Performance Testing

Technical components such as motors, fans and batteries are sourced from specialized manufacturers. Although technical specifications are provided by the manufacturers, it is common to verify these components in a lab environment as

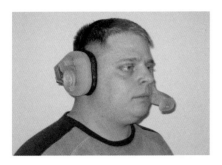

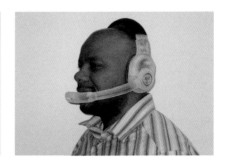

The comfort of each of the redesigned Motorola headsets for the NFL was verified through prototyping.

part of the engineering process. The testing may include a benchmark of competitors' components to compare performance and cost. This type of prototyping often requires the construction of test jigs and fixtures, which depending on the test and situation may require professional engineering involvement. The testing apparatus in this case is made to obtain repeatable and measurable quantitative data.

Safety Standards Testing

Product safety standards involve physical testing in a controlled laboratory environment. These standards are designed to protect consumers and are produced by organizations that specialize in assessing product risks and dangers. Standards organizations and independent testing labs will perform these tests for companies, to act as third-party validation. The tests simulate possible dangers, including impact, electrocution, strangulation or whatever hazards have been identified for the product category. The testing is done in highly controlled environments to ensure safety for the technicians and to have accurate results. Bicycle helmets, for example, are tested by dropping them on to anvils from a certain height in a drop tower. This simulates a person falling off a bike travelling a certain speed and hitting various objects.

This test set-up was built by FilterStream to test the suction of its hand-held vacuums. The amount of suction inside the box is measured while the vacuum is running to verify performance.

Prototyping in Different Disciplines

In closing it should be noted that product designers have to work with professionals from other disciplines where the term prototype could be used to describe many things that are not three-dimensional. Software designers use the term prototype in the context of code. Electronics engineers speak about prototyping printed circuit boards. Similarly, when an interaction designer speaks about a paper prototype, it is in reference to mocking-up screen interfaces for computers. When they speak about a wireframe they are referring to the layout of a website, whereas in product design this refers to lines in space that define the edges of a physical product in a CAD model. It is worthwhile becoming more aware of these semantic differences since product design has become inherently interdisciplinary.

This test set-up was built by Mixer Design Group to simulate and test the effect of a dog biting a pet toy. The metal rods and clamping pressure mimic the dog's mouth.

From Start to Finish: Comprehensive Case Studies

The use of prototypes will now be shown in the context of a few complete professional real-world design projects. As can be seen, the exact nature of the process will vary from organization to organization, as well as with the scope of the project. Student projects may last a few days or a whole year. In industry, projects could last for several years and be part of an ongoing product-development process.

Case Study Chair_ONE and Myto

The first explorations in creating Chair_ONE were in metal wire, but the final shape started to appear only when the work moved to paper.

A computer-constructed cardboard pattern (top) was followed by a laser-cut metal prototype (above).

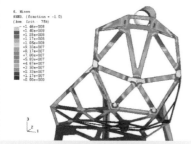

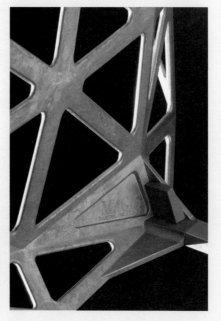

The final version of Chair_ONE was further developed through 3D CAD and utilized Finite Element Analysis for strength calculation.

The work of Munich-based Konstantin Grcic Industrial Design (KGID) spans a range of products, from furniture to kitchenware. Konstantin Grcic's chair designs have received particular acclaim, including Chair_ONE for Magis, and Myto, a cantilevered plastic chair created in collaboration with BASF and the furniture manufacturer Plank.

In exploring design solutions, Grcic's process moves back and forth between drawing, computer and quick prototypes. There is a playfulness and curiosity in the early prototypes that is focused yet experimental. Grcic gives many reasons when asked about the importance of making prototypes. For one, he has observed that when someone is building something physical, other people tend to gather around and give creative input more readily than when someone is working on the computer. Quick explorative prototypes can be examined, destroyed and then reconstructed quickly. This is a form of iteration that necessitates that neither the prototype nor the design be seen as 'too precious' early on. Instead the focus is on learning, keeping the prototypes at what he terms 'an appropriate level'. He employs all kinds of materials and approaches in building his prototypes, depending on what is being tested.

In the development of the award-winning Chair_ONE for the company Magis, the challenge was to design a chair entirely out of aluminium as one die-cast part. The initial explorations started with bent wire in order to create the semblance of an all-metal chair. It was only when he started experimenting with cardboard that the true shape of the chair started taking form.

'Chair_ONE is constructed just like a football: a number of flat planes assembled at angles to each other, creating the three-dimensional form.' (Böhm 2005) This allowed the design to be created as simple planes on the computer that could be printed out and used as templates for cardboard prototypes. Once proportions had been explored, the same templates could be used to laser-cut metal for a presentation model to Magis. The final design still needed to be translated into a die-cast aluminium part. The final design was done in 3D CAD, which also allowed Finite Element Analysis tools to be used for design verification prior to creating the die-cast tooling.

The Myto cantilevered plastic chair was created to demonstrate the structural possibilities of a plastic material made by BASF called Ultradur® thermoplastic polyester. A cantilevered plastic chair presents a problem for ordinary plastic materials, as they would tend to bend or crack over time. Glass-reinforced Ultradur®, on the other hand, offered the required structural possibilities. The chair needed to be attractive and strong, yet springy, since that is a fundamental enjoyment of sitting in a cantilevered chair.

An early prototype for the Myto chair made from cardboard and perforated sheet metal was used to explore the overall form factor and design strategy. This model was reverse-engineered into CAD using measurements.

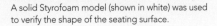

A solid Styrofoam model (shown in white) was used to verify the shape of the seating surface.

A final prototype of the Myto chair was made using the laser-sintering process. This prototype receives some final tweaks before the production tooling is made.

The first prototypes were made out of cardboard and perforated sheet metal. These explored the construction strategy of creating one solid form that was separated into a thick frame-bearing section with a thinner perforated seating surface. Extra strength could be added to the frame-bearing portion if necessary, making the design strategy more flexible. This model was then reverse-engineered by physical measurement back into the computer.

A solid Styrofoam prototype with a supporting core was useful in verifying the seat shape and ergonomic comfort. The seat surface was covered with tape to explore and communicate different perforation patterns.

Achieving a balance between functional comfort and strength required further prototyping and verification. The 3D CAD model was used both to run FEA simulation and to output a full-scale 3D rapid prototype. This laser-sintered prototype did not have the strength of the final Ultradur® but allowed the designers to understand the chair's behaviour and make some final tweaks to the design. The final production chair could be further tweaked by changing the material composition, which in fact was minimal given the extensive verification that preceded it.

Case Study ECOtality Blink Range of Electric Vehicle Chargers

The ECOtality line of Blink electric vehicle chargers includes a wall-mounted residential charger (left), a pedestal commercial charger (top) and a commercial DC fast-charging station (above). Each of the three different types of use had to be considered in its own context.

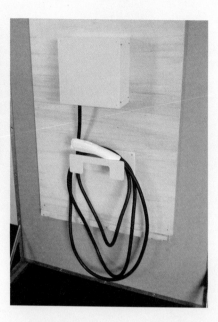

Low-fidelity full-scale prototypes were useful for user testing and showed that the residential cable wrap should be kept very close to the wall and separate from the charger housing.

This case study showcases the work of Frog Design of San Francisco working in partnership with ECOtality, a company specializing in clean electric transport technologies, to develop its range of three different 'Blink' charging stations for electric vehicles. It not only illustrates the importance of real physical prototyping throughout the design process, but also shows how the prototyping needs and methods may vary based on the intended environment and specific issues for each product. According to design director Howard Nuk at Frog, 'Physical experimentation (in-studio and on location) was the only way to both challenge and prove our theories. For each of the three chargers, we created a series of models to test specific usability, structural and aesthetic hypotheses.' The context of each product is different, even though the products are all chargers.

The first of the three chargers was a wall-mounted unit designed for private garages or carports. Secondly, a pedestal-mounted charger was designed for multiple installations across carparks. Lastly, a larger commercial unit, designed to fit between two parking spaces in a petrol station environment or in front of a superstore, was developed for fast-charging a vehicle in about 20 minutes.

All these environments had to be studied and understood in detail, requiring extensive exploration and investigation using models.

For the wall-mounted residential unit, a full-scale foamboard mock-up was created in the studio. This was instrumental in gaining two insights

that would influence the product's configuration in this environment. The first observation was that garage spaces are tight and consequently the charger's profile had to be kept as close as possible to the wall. The second was that constraining the cable wrap to the charger housing (like almost every wall-mounted charger to date) had a series of functional limitations. The cable wrap was instead made into a separate entity, allowing the customer to mount it closer to the electric vehicle charging port while keeping the charger housing and touch screen at a more comfortable eye level. Simple low-fidelity models of the charger were used to act out scenarios and to confirm the proper design configuration.

Electric vehicle chargers operate with thick copper wire. This raised many questions about functionality. Would users find the cable heavy? How far can a cable be conveniently pulled? What would happen when the temperature fell below freezing and the copper hardened?

To address such questions, the team froze cabling to understand bend radii and manoeuvrability, mocked-up parking/charging situations of all kinds and even devised weighted pulley systems to test cable weight management.

For the pedestal-mounted unit, it was critical to understand how the design would be suitable to the many different types of environment around shopfronts and carparks. Taking photographs and creating layouts of various real-life configurations allowed the team to examine the flexibility of installation.

Simple scale models examined different means by which to alleviate some of the fast-charger cable weight from the user's hands. Simple models help people visualize ideas and aid discussion among team members.

For the fast charger, the primary issue was the size and weight of the charging cable. In order to achieve the 20-minute charge, the cables needed to be almost twice the weight of the other charger units. Different solutions were brainstormed and visualized as small-scale models. These were useful for discussion and enabled the team to discount complex and unworkable ideas from the start. Instead, they chose a simpler strategy that suspended the cables from a high point, thereby reducing the resultant lifting force.

As the design of all three configurations progressed, high-fidelity appearance models were produced to complement 3D CAD virtual models. These physical models were used for final assessment of aesthetics (including colour, material, finish and proportion), as well as for media purposes via photos, videos and live conferences and exhibitions.

3D CAD allowed designers to create numerous detailed design iterations. Computer renderings were complemented with real physical prototypes made in high-density modelling board (page 122) that could be evaluated in their intended environment.

In order to evaluate the design in its proper physical context, models could not be judged in the studio alone. Howard Nuk points out that the 'product's proportions can often be misjudged due to artificial lighting, confined spaces and ceilings. Taking our DC fast-charger model to the intended install location to be judged among other devices like gas pumps and water/air pumps, and the infinite ceiling of the sky, gave the designers (and clients) a true understanding of the product's impression.'

A 360-degree lighting beacon on top of the pedestal charger allows drivers to locate it in a carpark at night. The light quality of the LEDs was extensively studied with prototypes.

Models were evaluated in real environments in order to verify and tweak the design.

Case Study Xoran Portable xCAT Scanner

Medical companies often focus on their core technology and look to design companies to assist with product design and development. Xoran Technologies turned to Insight Product Development in Chicago for help with the development of a mobile CT scanner using Xoran's compact CT scan technology. This new product would allow doctors to monitor patients directly in the operating room rather than only before and after surgical procedures.

Several specific design requirements needed to be investigated and verified through prototyping. The first was the space limitation for a mobile imaging device in an already cramped operating room. The scanner also had to be easily manoeuvered by one nurse in this environment. The primary engineering requirement was that the scanner had to be able to perform rotational imaging with very little vibration. Imaging during surgery meant that a unique user interface with an integrated keyboard and image monitor would have to be developed. Additionally the keyboard and monitor needed to be easily accessible during surgery.

An initial computer model showed that there was enough room to move the device around the patient in the operating room.

User testing, however, had to be conducted in the real environment in order to verify that a nurse was able comfortably and effectively to move the machine in the intended environment. A full-scale weighted non-working physical prototype was used for this purpose as well as to map

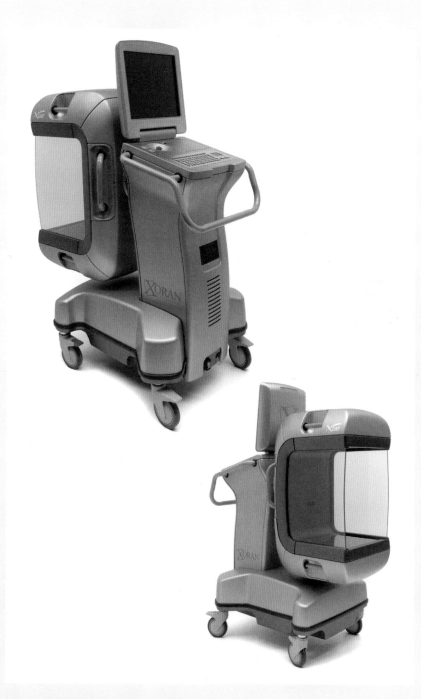

The Xoran portable xCAT® scanner is designed to be used inside the operating room to allow physicians to monitor patients during surgery.

A non-working physical prototype was employed to verify many usage requirements in a real setting.

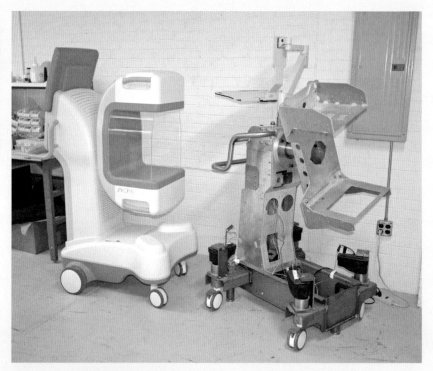

Looks-like versus works-like prototype of the frame.

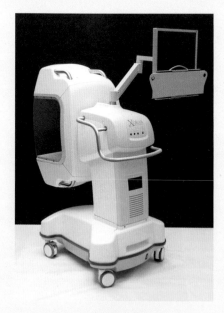

Second-generation verification prototype used to explore the articulating arm concept versus the final design iteration with folding monitor.

out the operational tasks for the graphical user interface for the device.

This looks-like prototype was complemented with works-like prototypes to verify mechanical functionality and imaging requirements for the rotational mechanism.

A second-generation prototype incorporated more detailed design requirements, but was also used to verify that an articulating monitor arm was unnecessary. This in turn led to further design iterations in order to incorporate a more compact keyboard and fold-down monitor into the overall design. At this point it was also decided that the product should have a much more dynamic and automotive appearance in order to appeal to the intended market as well as to stand out from other stationary products in the

same environment. This is evident in the final metallic colour choices. The xCAT® won a Medical Design Excellence Gold Award in 2008. Prototyping was a key design strategy in the development of this new medical product. It was used to explore options, test user experiences and verify many different design issues. Given the small production volumes of such highly specialized machines, the final prototypes were also used for device approval and for first-generation sales.

Case Study Tana Water Bar

The Tana Water Bar is a water appliance that sits on a worktop, connected to the water main, and both filters and chills or heats drinking water. The form, designed by NewDeal Design of San Francisco as the silhouette of a vase, was meant to evoke in an understated way a natural form of a water vessel.

During the initial part of the project NewDeal designers researched the issues that were important for the design of the product. This established certain requirements, such as where it would be used, by whom (target audience), price point and other important marketing and performance objectives.

An approved brief and understanding of the product's intended use formed the basis for ideation. The designers covered the walls with sketches, both in order to communicate their ideas and to help identify issues for further design development.

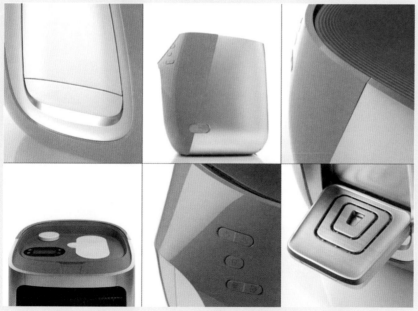

The Tana Water Bar is a sophisticated water filtration and heating or cooling water appliance.

NewDeal designers collaborated to fill an entire wall with different ideas for the product. At this stage anything goes and forms the basis for exploration.

The best ideas were combined and distilled into the preferred conceptual direction.

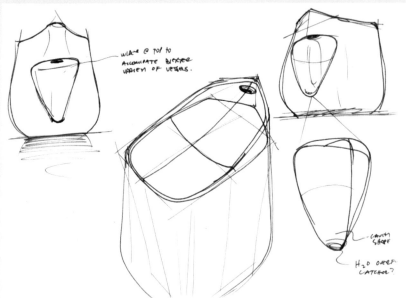

The initial ideas were reviewed and then refined into successively more focused concepts.

After reviewing the initial sketch and model explorations with the client, the design team received enough feedback and direction to start the next step of the process. The objective of this step would be to define one design direction, so as to start focusing toward a solution. The aim was to develop a very precise and plausible design, including all technical constraints and inputs.

This required a more precise drawing approach and a layout of the internal components in 3D CAD so that

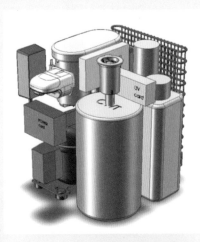

The inner workings were first modelled in 3D CAD to give a realistic size and overall form factor, which the designers could then draw around.

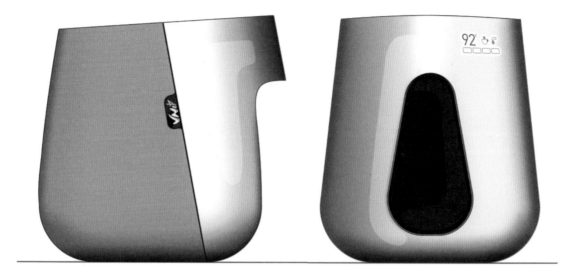

Two-dimensional elevations gave an idea of what the product would look like.

the overall form could be developed on top of the internal configuration in full scale.

Elevation views gave a good idea of the visual and sculptural design intent, and were complemented with physical low-fidelity prototypes in polystyrene foam based on these two-dimensional layouts. The 3D polystyrene models gave a much clearer idea of the overall proportions and what the water-dispensing area should look like at the front. The models were thus used to explore the form in more detail.

Explorative handmade models in polystyrene foam allowed the designers to explore the form in more detail.

The polystyrene foam model was scanned into 3D and formed the basis for the final form factor.

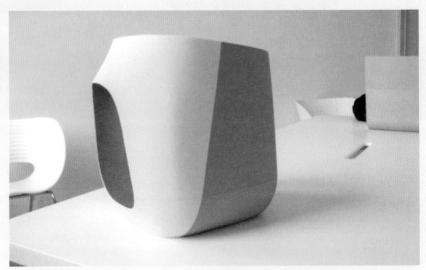

The first set of appearance models focused on the overall form factor and proportions. They were accurately machined on a CNC to be suitable for presentation to a wider audience.

Final high-fidelity appearance prototypes took the design to the next level, examining every aspect of the product's detailing. The design went through two final iterations of refinement and physical prototyping to communicate and verify design details.

PROTOTYPING INTERACTIVE ELECTRONIC PRODUCTS

3

Electronics are ubiquitous and are found in a variety of products, including consumer electronics, medical systems, toys and even soft goods (textile products). Products therefore increasingly incorporate a growing list of interactive technologies, including: screen-based interfaces, keypads, wireless elements and sensors.

In the previous chapter it was shown how interactive elements could be tested initially with simple low-fidelity prototypes by investigating scenarios. Screen-based interfaces can, for example, be acted out step by step with a paper prototype. This can then progress into higher-fidelity prototypes on screen using programs such as Powerpoint® or Flash®. Beyond screen-based interfaces, it may be important to have the prototypes work so that instead of scenarios being acted out, they can actually be experienced through real sensors and output. New simple toolkits to explore interactive product ideas in the form of works-like prototypes have become increasingly popular and accessible. What is particularly attractive is that they do not require an extensive knowledge of electronic design. These tools are used as a proof of concept to make sure the ideas are viable and to investigate the benefit for the end user. The focus here is not on electronics design, but on prototyping the experience. Design students have several toolkits at their disposal. Lego Mindstorms® is a robotic kit from Lego® with a number of sensors that can be used to detect sound, motion and range, which in turn can be translated into specific outputs such as motion and light.

More elaborate prototyping platforms have also become available that specifically target the artist and designer. Arduino is an open-source electronics prototyping platform that can be used to create interactive products. Software can be downloaded from the open-source site www.arduino.cc, along with instructions on where to purchase the boards. The Arduino board also uses sensors and is able to drive outputs. The small and inexpensive boards can also be incorporated more easily into working prototypes than the bulkier Lego® system.

Lego Mindstorms® NXT is a stand-alone controller with an easily programmable interface. A variety of sensors, including touch, infrared, range and sound, can be used to produce output including servomotors. It is programmed through a computer.

The Smart Rollator project at Carleton University, Ottawa, used Lego Mindstorms® and a range of prototyping platforms such as Arduino open-source software.

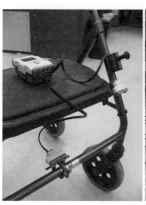

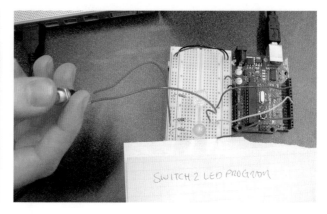

Case Study Kurio Interactive Museum Guide

Kurio is a museum guide system designed to enhance interaction among family members and small groups visiting the museum. The Kurio system allows visitors to choose from a range of interactive scenarios - in one scenario a family imagines themselves as time travelers whose time map is broken and so they are lost in the present time. In order to repair the time map, family members complete missions comprised of a series of challenges to collect information from the museum helping to reconstruct the map. The interactive museum guide itself is comprised of four tangible devices, a tabletop display, and a personal digital assistant (PDA) all networked wirelessly to a central reasoning engine that guides the family through the museum visit.

TANGIBLE PROTOTYPES

POINTING DEVICE   FINDING DEVICE   TEXT DEVICE   LISTENING DEVICE

Kurio is an interactive museum guide system designed for small groups visiting the museum. It is comprised of four hand-held devices, a tabletop display and a Personal Digital Assistant (PDA), all networked wirelessly to a central reasoning engine that guides the family through the museum visit.

The Kurio interactive museum guide system is the outcome of a collaborative research project between Simon Fraser University, Surrey, British Columbia and Carleton University, Ottawa, Ontario. The case study highlights how low-fidelity prototypes and more complex high-fidelity working electronic prototypes may be used in the same project. The objective was to use technology to enhance interaction among family members in the museum setting. Existing museum guides typically use audio or a Personal Digital Assistant (PDA) to guide the visitor through a museum setting. The problem is that this tends to isolate family members from one another and thus detracts from social interaction and learning.

The Kurio system is very different. It uses a set of four different wireless hand-held devices to create a socially interactive game where family members collaborate in collecting different types of information in a museum setting. The four collecting devices are easy to operate and simply have one button. They include a pointer (for pointing to an artefact), a listener (for collecting sounds), a finder for guiding users around the museum and a reader (for capturing text). These devices are coordinated through a PDA screen-based device that is operated by a parent.

The system was not envisioned like this at the beginning of the project, which took about three years to complete. It emerged as a result of observing and studying families interact in real and simulated museum settings. The process was made possible through prototyping that started with simple low-fidelity models to investigate early scenarios, followed by more elaborate looks-like models that were tested in a simulated museum environment. Finally, full working prototypes were made that were used in museum field trials.

Screen-based interfaces were tested with simple paper prototypes, which was an effective approach for investigating button layouts and other physical interactive elements. Important insights were gained from these tests even though the devices did not actually work.

All this initial learning was critical to creating the design specifications. These included the decision that the devices needed to have an appearance that was metaphoric in terms of the tool's purpose. This was a key insight, since it meant a different device for each specific task. The reader tool, for example, looks like a magnifying glass, while the way-finder tool looks like a Y-shaped divining rod. The earlier

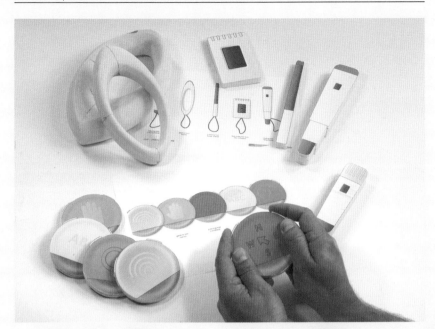

Explorative prototypes were made in foamboard and Styrofoam to allow team members to develop interaction scenarios that could be studied further.

A simulated museum exhibit served as a setting for initial user testing of non-working prototypes by groups of families.

models also showed that the children had a preference for larger and brightly coloured devices. The final working prototypes made use of prototyping electronic kits and 3D printed parts. These included a variety of sensors as well as wireless technology, all available in prototyping kit formats. The final museum field trial was a proof of concept that illustrated the benefits of interactive play to create a more interactive and social learning experience in a museum setting for families.

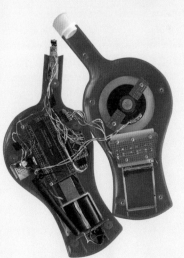

Kurio hand-held museum guide: high-fidelity working prototypes with electronics.

MODELMAKING

PRINCIPLES AND CHOICES FOR MODELMAKING

In order to build the right kind of model it helps first to consider the guiding principles that apply to any modelmaking effort. These will in turn help to guide the choices of materials as well as process.

Principles of Modelmaking

These principles are in essence the rules that one should try to consider before, and while, making the models. These help to keep the big picture in mind, which in turn will make the experience more effective, useful and safe.

Health and Safety

Nothing is more important than safety. Please read Chapter 5 on health and safety (page 45) and never attempt to use any machine tools without the proper training and supervision. Always wear the appropriate safety clothing and equipment, read the instructions and study the safety data sheets for materials.

Purpose

The model is built to serve the prototyping uses outlined in the Prototyping section of Chapters 1 to 3. Looks-like models will usually be built in a solid form. This means that since there are no internal functional parts, the model will not be cored out. This is faster and sufficient for the end purpose. Similarly, a prototype built for the purpose of testing a mechanical function can be made more easily by not worrying too much about the exterior appearance. It is therefore often more economical to build separate models to examine appearance versus function. This also requires some discipline. It is easy to get drawn into the temptation of building something that comes as close to the final product as possible, losing sight of the fact that the model was meant only to explore or test one aspect of the design.

Effectiveness

Models should be built in an effective way. It is useful to reflect on the requirements by asking some introspective questions. How precise does the model need to be? A lower level of precision may be faster and more economical, and acceptable for the intended purpose. Can the model serve several uses, or is it quicker and easier to build separate models to look at different issues? What is faster? What is easier to change? Also use the computer effectively. Is this the time to start designing the final product in 3D, or can the computer be used more efficiently as a tool for making templates for some quick handmade models?

Appropriateness

There is a difference between a model built for exploration and one built to persuade clients and investors about the value of a concept. The former can be rough and purposeful by virtue of its content, whereas the latter needs to be viewed in a formal light. Both models could be built to a low level of fidelity, but the workmanship and level of finish of a model for presentation to non-designers generally needs to be perfect. To an outside eye, a model with exposed glue marks and poor workmanship might create an impression of lack of professionalism and credibility. On the other hand, a model being built for a presentation does not necessarily need to be painted and finished to the level of the final product, as this could create the impression that the design is further ahead than intended. The audience and venue are therefore important factors to be considered.

Choices to Consider

By considering and following the above guidelines you will be able to make better choices in both materials and process. There are always options when making a model and there is never going to be a single perfect right answer. The important thing is to think through your objectives and base your decisions on the guiding principles.

Materials

In prototypes, materials of mass production are typically substituted for simpler and easier-to-work-with materials and processes. This obviously has to be taken into consideration both functionally and visually. Simple materials such as foamboard and paper might be suitable for making explorative models that can be created safely and quickly. At some point these materials reach their potential, and the next iteration progresses to stronger and more exact materials. This does not mean that the material has to be exact in terms of the intended material of manufacture; a solid piece of high-density polyurethane foam can be finished and painted to look like an injection-moulded part. Modelmaking materials often used in product design will be outlined in detail in the following chapters with step-by-step examples.

Another aspect of material selection is experimentation. In order to realize new design possibilities you need to try new things, including new materials. Relying solely on known materials will limit your design possibilities. The materials shown in this book serve as a basis for formal and functional exploration. It is important to complement this with explorations into new materials that need to be examined for their innovative virtues, such as sustainability.

Take some time to experiment with safer, water-based materials if you are still using solvent-based paints and fillers. You still need to understand how to identify chemical hazards that may be hidden in a water-based product (see Chapter 5, page 47).

Tools

Some materials are worked easily with hand tools, whereas others require power or machine tools. The use of machine tools requires proper training and professional supervision. Many design firms and other professional settings do not have such facilities. In practice, machined parts can therefore be subcontracted to modelmaking shops. The precision offered by mills and lathes is usually not required for quicker exploration work that forms the mainstay of in-house prototyping activity. Digital methods such as 3D printing are cleaner and safer alternatives to machining, and are increasingly commonplace in both schools and companies.

HEALTH AND SAFETY

Goal

Modelmaking has the potential to expose students to hazardous materials, processes and equipment. This includes, but is not limited to, mechanical machinery, sharp tools, dust, various materials and chemicals, noise and fire hazards. Increasingly, artists and designers are being made aware of the hidden dangers and long-term chronic effects of some of the ingredients in artist materials. It is a goal of this book to make people think twice about what they are doing when modelmaking, in terms of their own safety and that of those around them. This chapter can serve only as a basic overview of health and safety for the following reasons:

1. Entire books are dedicated to this subject, some of which are listed at the end of this chapter.
2. Universities and art schools typically have their own health and safety committees, which set their own procedures and rules.
3. Health and safety laws and regulations differ between and even within countries. They can affect you differently depending on whether you are an employee, a student or a hobbyist.
4. Rules and regulations keep evolving.
5. People are likely to use different materials and processes from those outlined in the book, which, for example, does not cover metal or ceramics.

At the same time it should be the student's objective to become knowledgeable in the materials and tools of use in order to be aware of any potential hazards. Consult with your department and your health and safety committee for additional training about safety. Government and other safety organization websites may be consulted for additional up-to-date information. Although not exhaustive, a set of links have been provided at the end of this chapter.

Hazards

Low-fidelity materials and processes generally require simple tools and can be carried out on a desktop. Other approaches require much more attention to safety, especially where they involve machines and chemical materials. Choose the safest materials and tools whenever possible. Although every attempt has been made to suggest safer ways of working and safer materials, the list of manufacturers and products at the end of the book does not constitute any form of safety endorsement – a list of potential hazards exists whenever working with any art materials and tools. The first step is to be aware of the types of hazards and the necessary precautions. For your convenience a system of Safety Checks is highlighted at the beginning of Chapters 6 to 20 as a starting point.

Mechanical Hazards

Tools and machines present a mechanical hazard. Tools should not be used for anything except their designed function as they might break and cause injury in the process. They should be kept in proper working condition for the same reason. It is also important to keep a clean workspace. Sharp tools hidden below a mass of parts and dirt pose a hazard in and of themselves. Obstacles, dirt and tools left carelessly on the floor also create a tripping hazard. In addition, a clean environment makes one more aware of one's surroundings.

You should never operate any equipment while under the influence of alcohol, drugs or lack of sleep. Competence is a critical aspect of any tool operation and you should have proper training and supervision. For machine tools this automatically implies professional training and supervision by a certified technician. Machine tools are very powerful and have the potential to cause serious permanent injury or death. It is important to make sure that machine safety shields are in place before using such machinery. Common power and machine shop tools are reviewed in Chapter 8 of this book (pp. 58–62), along with some general safety preparation procedures for power and machine tools, as well as more specific safety issues for different types of machines. Always be sure to wear appropriate safety gear, including safety glasses and hearing protection, which are outlined at the end of this chapter. Always use common sense.

Hazardous Substances

Hazardous substances enter the body through inhalation, absorption through the skin or ingestion through oral cavities. They include chemicals often found in uncured glues, paints and fillers or casting compounds. They can also be released through sanding in the form of dust, or when a material is burnt or melted. Dust may include fine wood fibres or silica from filler. Solvents release vapours and polystyrene foam can release harmful gases when melted with a hotwire. Some chemicals become more dangerous if mixed together because they might react. It is therefore important to understand how to safeguard oneself through prevention, control and protection.

Inhalation is generally prevented through adequate ventilation. This requires that contaminated air be removed in a direction away from the user so that the user only breathes clean air. An open window is not sufficient. Spray booths and fume hoods should therefore be used whenever chemicals are mixed or spray painting is being performed. For woodworking and other dust generation a proper dust-collection system should be employed.

Absorption typically happens through the skin. This is why common sense dictates to keep chemicals away from your body. Lab coats (or other appropriate clothing) should be worn when handling materials with chemicals in them, as well as appropriate safety gloves (see below) and chemical goggles.

With regard to ingestion it is important not to eat or drink in the environment where modelmaking is taking place or when working with chemical materials. You should remove your lab coat and wash your hands before eating.

Three different adverse health effects arise from exposure:

1. Sensitization
2. Acute (short-term) reactions
3. Chronic (long-term) reactions

Sensitization is an allergic reaction to a certain material. Once sensitized, a person can no longer tolerate exposure to the material. This can happen quickly or over a longer period of time and will affect each person differently.

Chemicals can cause acute reactions. These typically appear quickly, such as a burn, dizziness, nausea or other noticeable ailment. If such a reaction occurs, you should stop the activity immediately and seek medical attention.

Chronic exposures can be very serious, but may take months or years to develop. Unfortunately some chronic hazards are still not completely understood. What is of particular concern to health experts is that new chemicals are being created without knowing if there are chronic long-term effects. This is why it is so important to use common sense and to treat all materials as potentially toxic and protect oneself at all times. People may react differently based on their body size, age and medical history. A person who has a medical condition, such as asthma or skin rashes for example, can suffer a more adverse reaction than someone who does not. The effect of exposure also varies with the amount and frequency of exposure.

The Environment

Disposal and clean-up are issues that have to be taken into consideration. Make sure to follow the disposal requirements and laws that pertain to the materials you are using.

Cautionary Labelling and Safety Data Sheets (SDS)

It is not enough to assume that because you buy a material from an art, hobby or DIY shop, the material is safe. The only way to know for certain is to study and understand the chemicals contained in the product. Water-based products are usually preferable to products containing organic solvents. This is because most organic solvents are flammable and can also cause a range of adverse chronic health effects, especially over time and with prolonged use. In addition, solvent-based products typically require additional solvents for thinning and clean-up, thereby increasing exposure. Water-based products may still contain acute as well as chronic hazards, so precautions must be taken.

Consumer products should have labels that identify immediate hazards such as flammability (indicating solvents) and poison. Read the labels; the toxicity cannot be determined by smell. Keep all materials safely stored and away from children.

Workplace hazardous materials require proper labels and additional health and safety information in the form of Safety Data Sheets (SDS). Different countries have different names and requirements for these documents. In the United Kingdom, Control of Substances Hazardous to Health (COSHH) data sheets are often used and in North America they are known as Material Safety Data Sheets (MSDS). The international Safety Data Sheet (SDS) format was adopted by the UN Economic and Social Council and utilizes the Globally Harmonized System of classification and labelling of chemicals (GHS). This contains a list of 16 items of materials and associated safety information. For a more detailed explanation, please refer to the GHS link in the resources at the end of this book.

Contents of a 16 Heading SDS Sheet

Heading	Brief Description
1. Identification	The product's intended purpose and name, e.g. 'Arts and Crafts, Basic Gesso'.
2. Composition	The chemical ingredients, e.g. 'polystyrene with HFC blowing agent' for Styrofoam.
3. Hazard Identification	This section lists inhalation, skin contact and ingestion hazards.
4. First Aid Measures	In case of accidental exposure.
5. Fire Fighting Measures	This information is for emergency fire response.
6. Accidental Release Measures	Instructions for accidental spills, etc.

7. Handling and Storage	Includes rules for personal handling, such as 'do not inhale or expose to skin', and for storage, such as to keep in a well-ventilated space.
8. Exposure Controls – Personal Protection	Manufacturer's recommendation for personal protective equipment.
9. Physical and Chemical Properties	Describes the physical nature of the product, e.g. flash point, evaporation rate.
10. Stability and Reactivity	Warnings about mixing this material with any other chemicals or exposing to heat sources etc. Reactivity hazards: for example, mixing ammonia and household bleach will result in the release of a harmful gas.
11. Toxicological Information	Informs you about possible effects of exposure and symptoms.
12. Ecological Information	For example, is the product biodegradable?
13. Disposal	This varies from country to country. Be aware of local jurisdictions.
14. Transportation	Any specific transportation requirements.
15. Regulatory Information	For example, EU regulations.
16. Other	

Person wearing safety glasses with side shields (top) and goggles (above).

Personal Protective Equipment

The risk of exposure should always be minimized. This means removing the hazards as much as possible through engineering controls such as spray-booth systems and fume hoods for ventilation, and dust-collection systems for woodworking or sanding any material.

Eye Protection

Safety glasses protect against sharp or flying objects and should always be worn when using machinery or sharp instruments that could accidentally break; they are therefore routinely required in any student laboratories or workshops. Sealed goggles are designed to protect against chemicals and provide a seal.

Dust Masks

Dust masks should be worn to provide extra protection against airborne dust from sanding various materials, including the polystyrene foam, polyurethane foam, plastic and wood materials described in this book. They are not a substitute for adequate ventilation and a proper dust-collection system. They are not designed to provide protection against fine particulates or chemical vapours.

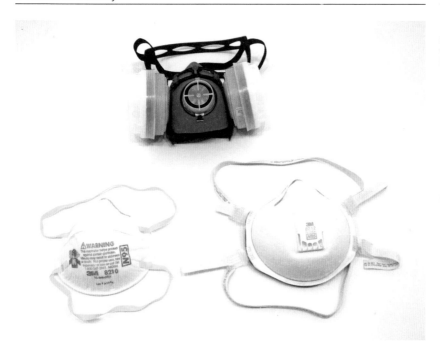

Respirators come in different styles and offer protection against different hazards. Anyone considering the need for a respirator should have a health check and seek professional help.

Respirators

The best protection from airborne particulates and chemical hazards is from spray booths and fume hoods. Health and safety literature advises that respirators are the last line of defence. Anyone considering the need for a respirator should have a health check and seek professional training and advice in the selection of a respirator. At schools this typically starts with the health and safety committee and shop personnel.

Employers are required to adhere to stringent rules and laws when it comes to respirators. Wearing a respirator requires health evaluation, fit testing and monitoring, and hence a proper respiratory programme. This is because they can create problems for people with asthma or other medical conditions and may not offer adequate protection if they are not worn, fitted and maintained properly. There are many different types of respirator designed to filter or absorb different types of particulates and vapours. The respirator needs to be matched specifically to the type of hazard being protected against in order to work effectively.

Rubber gloves come in different materials and should be inspected for tears before use.

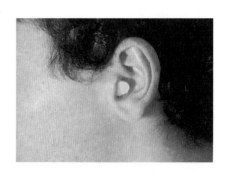

Disposable Gloves

Disposable gloves are made of various types of material, including latex, nitrile and neoprene. These need to be worn when handling and using chemical materials. Some people are allergic to latex. Read the manufacturer's SDS sheet when working with materials to select proper glove type. If the sheet is unspecific, call the manufacturer. Gloves should be inspected for tears before use and discarded after use.

Earplugs and earmuffs are worn around any noisy equipment.

Ear Protection

Excessive noise for extended periods can cause damage to hearing, including hearing loss and tinnitus (prolonged ringing in the ear). Earplugs are simple to wear and should be worn around noisy equipment. They are custom-moulded to the ear channel. Earmuffs offer more sound protection.

Further Health and Safety Resources

The author and Laurence King Publishing cannot take any responsibility for what is listed in the websites or books cited.

3M, from *Guidance for Establishing a Respiratory Protection Program* (n.d.), from http://solutions.3m.com/wps/portal/3M/en_US/Health/Safety/Products/Two/ (retrieved 28 Jan, 2011)

Canadian Centre for Occupational Health and Safety, *The MSDS: A Basic Guide For Users – International Version* (n.d.), from http://ccinfoweb.ccohs.ca/help/msds/msdsINTGUIDE.html (retrieved 25 Jan, 2011)

Health Canada, *Aim for Safety, Target the Label* (Fact Sheet) (n.d.), from http://www.hc-sc.gc.ca/cps-spc/pubs/cons/label-letiquette-eng.php (retrieved 27 Jan, 2011)

Health Canada, *Workplace Hazardous Materials Information System* (n.d.), from http://www.hc-sc.gc.ca/ewh-semt/occup-travail/whmis-simdut/index-eng.php (retrieved 27 Jan, 2011)

Hughes, P., and L. Hughes, *Easy Guide to Health and Safety*, Oxford: Elsevier (2008)

McCann, M.P., and A. Babin, *Health Hazards Manual for Artists* (6th edn.), USA: Lyons Press (2008)

Occupational Safety and Health Administration (US Department of Labor), *A Guide to The Globally Harmonized System of Classification and Labelling of Chemicals* (n.d.), from http://www.osha.gov/dsg/hazcom/ghs.html#1.0 (retrieved 27 Jan, 2011)

Occupational Safety and Health Administration (US Department of Labor), *Respiratory Protection* (n.d.), from http://www.osha.gov/pls/oshaweb/owadisp.show_document?p_table=STANDARDS&p_id=12716 (retrieved 28 Jan, 2011)

Rossol, M., *The Artist's Complete Health and Safety Guide* (3rd edn.), New York, Allworth Press (2001)

US Consumer Product Safety Commission, *Art and Craft Safety Guide* (n.d.), from http://www.cpsc.gov/cpscpub/pubs/art.html (retrieved 25 Jan, 2011)

Clothing and Footwear, Hair and Jewellery

Loose-fitting clothing and jewellery have to be removed, as they could potentially become entangled in machinery. Long hair is an extreme hazard for the same reason and must therefore be tied back and covered where necessary. Proper clothing such as a lab coat can provide some skin protection against some chemical materials. Machine shop coats or aprons are worn to provide protection against dirt and oil, but should also be worn properly so that there is no chance of them getting caught in moving machinery. Shoes should completely cover and shield the foot in order to provide protection against dropped objects or chemicals.

Risk Assessment

All work should start with a personal assessment of risk. This includes understanding the safety aspects discussed above and taking the time to read safety data sheets and instruction labels. It also means wearing appropriate clothing and proper protective equipment for the job at hand.

Never take any chances or rush; be patient. Never play around tools or dangerous environments; it is distracting both to yourself and others, and such behaviour can cause accidents. Also start by doing an inspection of the work area for any hidden dangers. Areas around mechanical machinery should be kept clean of debris and dirt that could cause you to trip or slip. Also be aware of your surroundings, including people in your vicinity. A visual inspection is also required to ensure that the machinery is sound and properly secured to either the floor or workbench. Any strange noises emanating from machinery indicates that you should turn them off and report the problem to a supervisor. Always consider safer methods or tools that would allow you to achieve the modelling objective. Seek professional advice if any doubt exists as to the safety of either equipment or procedure; the role of the model-shop technician is to provide instructions for using the tools and equipment in a safe manner.

Above all, exercise caution and common sense. Never work alone or unsupervised. Overfamiliarity can also be a source of accidents, especially when work is done without thinking through the steps and being cautious.

SPACE AND SET-UP

Safety Check

— Read Chapter 5 on health and safety
— Students should follow school rules
— Do not allow clutter to take over your workspace
— Do not use paint, chemicals or solvent-based fillers in your personal workspace
— Store flammable or combustible materials safely

Space

There are a number of ways in which to construct models, which can be affected by the available space and environment. Some materials are suitable for use in small, simple workspaces, whereas others require substantial modelmaking facilities. Many professional design studios will have simple modelmaking facilities available for their designers to make models for early exploration and testing. They will then send out more advanced or higher-level-of-finish models to professional modelmaking shops. Usually the simple models made by the designers themselves far outnumber the more complex models and require much less complex tools and facilities. By the time the model is sent out the designer often has a good idea what he or she is looking for and the outsourced prototype is more or less made for verification or communication. Increasingly, design offices are adding 3D printing technology since the machines have become more affordable and easier to run.

Basic Set-Up

Work Surface

A good work surface is key to being able to do good work. The table should be clean and stable. Ideally, use a dedicated workbench: these have the required stability for sawing and filing a fixed workpiece. It is a good idea to have a replaceable top surface if the bench is used a lot. This can be as simple as a thin sheet of melamine or hardboard, which can easily be replaced when worn out. The work surface needs to be kept clean and smooth.

Vices

Vices are a simple and necessary part of working by hand with harder materials such as wood, high-density foam and metals. When sawing or filing these materials you need to ensure that they are fixed securely to a vice. Holding these materials in your hands while working on them will not provide enough resistance and is also unsafe.

Bench vices are securely attached with bolts to the workbench. They can usually tilt and rotate and have heavy jaws for securing the workpiece. You can also use soft jaws, which are inserts made in aluminium with rubber linings that prevent the workpiece from being marred.

The universal vice is a versatile and useful vice that is suitable for finer work. It is usually fitted with a suction cup to make it portable. Because it can be so well adjusted it works conveniently as an extra set of hands when doing fine detail work or sanding.

A sturdy bench vice provides secure holding of the workpiece (top), while a universal vice is useful for finer, more delicate work (above).

A magnifying work light provides both light and the ability to work in finer detail.

Dust may also be generated when working by hand. This is especially true when using modelling-foam materials, which cling to everything. It is important to keep the dust from accumulating by regularly vacuuming the area.

Lighting

Good lighting is an aspect of modelmaking that is often overlooked. It allows you to see better and therefore leads to better workmanship and level of detail. Good overall lighting can come from many sources, but for fine detail consider investing in a simple magnifying light. These are ideal for modelmaking and are readily available. The magnifying glass will come in handy when examining the model for detail.

Dust and Dirt Control

It is important to contain and collect dust that is generated from sanding. If any power tools are used some form of dust-collection system will be necessary. Depending on how much work is done, this will vary from using a wet/dry shop-type vacuum to a professional dust-collection system. If a wet/dry vacuum is used, then it should be fitted with a fine particle filter and provide adequate suction.

Work Habits

Try to develop good work habits. This is mostly common sense, but once bad habits are begun then they become ingrained. Good habits include:

— Cleaning up after yourself
— Paying close attention to health and safety
— Being respectful to anyone else sharing the space

WORKFLOW

7

Safety Check

— Read Chapter 5 on health and safety

Workflow is a systematic step-by-step process of creation. It applies to any skill, including sketching as well as modelmaking. It needs to be learnt, but with time becomes a natural process. Developing a good sense of workflow is perhaps the most critical aspect of improving your modelmaking skills. The experienced sketcher knows how to draw a perspective view of an idea with little effort. Similarly, the experienced musician is able to play the instrument as an extension of his or her own body. Prototyping is a similar type of skill, where practice will make it more natural and effective to go and build to explore, test, communicate and verify your designs. You will develop a sense of method and materials through practice. There is no formulaic or correct way of doing something, except for safety matters. This book serves as a foundation upon which new knowledge and experience can be built. There are many different modelmaking techniques and approaches, and you will learn new tips and tricks along the way.

When a piece of self-assembly furniture is purchased from a company such as IKEA, someone has already figured out the assembly workflow. The instruction manual guides the customer through the process of putting it all together and some tools are required. The aspiring designer needs to learn both how to make things and how to instruct other people to put them together. Modelmaking is a great way to become more familiar with materials, construction and assembly.

Basic Modelmaking Workflow

As a starting point consider the following basic approach to workflow:

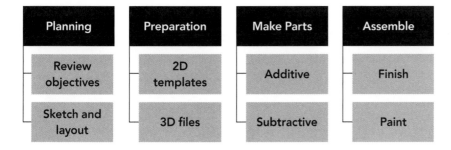

Planning	Preparation	Make Parts	Assemble
Review objectives	2D templates	Additive	Finish
Sketch and layout	3D files	Subtractive	Paint

Planning

The starting point for the model is usually a sketch or a simple computer drawing. The first step is to analyze the prototyping and modelmaking objectives, which involves two separate tasks. The first is to review what materials and processes are suitable by thinking through principles and choices (see Chapter 4, page 43). In early models this is typically a single material, while for more advanced prototypes several materials and processes tend to be combined.

The second task is to plan what pieces need to be made and how. For simpler, exploratory models this is a simpler and looser process. In essence the model, rather than the product, is being designed at this point. The model itself will be sketchy and much is worked out on the fly. For more advanced and higher-fidelity prototypes the drawings need to be more accurate and detailed in the form of a layout. This establishes the overall form and proportions as well as making sure that internal components fit. These prototypes should be drawn to scale in either

2D or 3D. Adobe Illustrator® and CorelDRAW® are typical drawing packages used to create 2D layouts. CAD programs such as AutoCAD®, Rhinoceros® and SolidWorks® allow for 2D as well as 3D layouts.

Preparation

Before making any pieces, it is necessary to create drawings or 3D files. 2D layouts can be printed on to paper and glued directly on to the modelling material as a pattern for cutting. This effective technique saves a great deal of time and helps with workmanship. The workflow examples in Chapters 11 and 12 on foamboard and foam show this in detail. Conversely, the layout can be used to create templates for outlines and cross sections. The templates can be used as sanding jigs or simply to check the profile of a surface.

Pieces can also be laid out in 3D, as needed for rapid prototyping or CNC machining. In this case the file will be created in a standard CAD program and exported in a file format that can be read by the rapid prototyping machine. This is typically an STL or IGS file format (see page 66).

Generally, layouts progress from 2D to 3D as the project advances. It is also common to mix handmade parts with rapid prototyping.

Making Parts

Subtractive modelling involves removing material from a solid block of material. Conversely, in additive modelling material is added bit by bit. This could be compared with carving a sculpture out of stone versus laying it up in clay. As a rule the additive approach is faster and more effective, since most forms are resultant combinations of basic geometric elements. One of the tricks behind modelmaking is to learn how to create essential pieces that can be glued together into the required shape. The best way to learn how to do this is through hands-on practical experience and modelmaking exercises. The step-by-step examples in this book will serve as a guide to that process.

Breaking the model into bits is also fundamentally different depending on whether you are making a looks-like or a works-like prototype. In the former it is important to model exterior forms and surfaces, recombining them into a final solid representation. In the latter it is a matter of breaking down the prototype into the required functional parts. In both cases this process starts with some sketching and quick planning and then progresses into more detailed sketches or full-scale templates.

Assembly

You should resist the temptation to assemble everything together before thinking through the finishing requirements. If parts are to be painted or finished in a different colour or texture, then it is better to keep them apart so they can be painted separately. Otherwise, masking will create a lot of extra work and invariably lead to worse results. Not all models are painted. Low-fidelity models tend to be left unpainted as this is appropriate, saves time and probably results in a cleaner model in the end. If the model is to be painted then you should choose the paints and colours carefully. It is best to paint parts prior to assembly in order to achieve a neater appearance.

If the model is simply made for show and tell then it may be wiser to not assemble parts permanently, just in case something needs to be tweaked or changed in the future. Sometimes a model is made with different configurations, so that one part can be swapped for another. This can be used to show a product in an open and closed state or to show variations.

Assembly of parts will therefore also depend on purpose. For works-like prototypes it is usually necessary to mechanically fasten parts together in a robust manner using screws and other hardware. In this case the exposed fastener may not look good, but that is probably of no consequence as it is only a works-like prototype. For looks-like prototypes it may be simpler and easier to glue parts together, even if that is not how they would be held together in production.

Reverse-Engineer Workflow

Complex sculptural forms often need to be developed by hand in such materials as clay or foam. Typical products that are modelled sculpturally include cars, helmets and character toys. The model then serves as a blueprint for the final form, which must be digitized in order to be brought into CAD.

Pictures and Measurements

A basic way of reverse-engineering a product is with a digital camera and some manual measurements. The workflow would be:

| Take pictures and measurements | Import pictures to 3D program | Construct 3D geometry |

Pictures can be scaled and brought into a 3D CAD program, where they serve as guides for the digital modelling. Some useful tips:

— Take pictures from side, top and front elevations and bring them into the computer system aligned on to these planes. This will form a good starting point for the model.
— Do not use a wide angle, and be careful of foreshortening. A picture taken further away will have less distortion. Align the camera to have a dead-on view.
— Include a ruler in the picture as a quick scale reference.

Konstantin Grcic reverse-engineered the first Myto chair prototype as a starting point for CAD.

The NextEngine stationary desktop scanner includes a rotating mounting base that automatically rotates the object to be scanned.

Measurements are typically made with a vernier caliper (see Chapter 8, page 58). It may be necessary to mark up the model in order to create reference points that can be traced back to the pictures. Consider using drafting tape as it is low-stick, marks well and can be removed afterward. As cross sections are created it is advisable to print them out on a piece of paper and cut out the profile to see if it fits on the model. This serves as an excellent guide.

Laser Scanning

Laser scanners are either hand-held or stationary. The hand-held scanners are suitable for scanning large surfaces, such as car bodies. A scanner can scan only what it sees. This means that either the operator needs to move around the object during the scanning process or else the object needs to move relative to the scanner. Hand-held scanners follow the first principle, whereas stationary scanners need to combine several scans from different views.

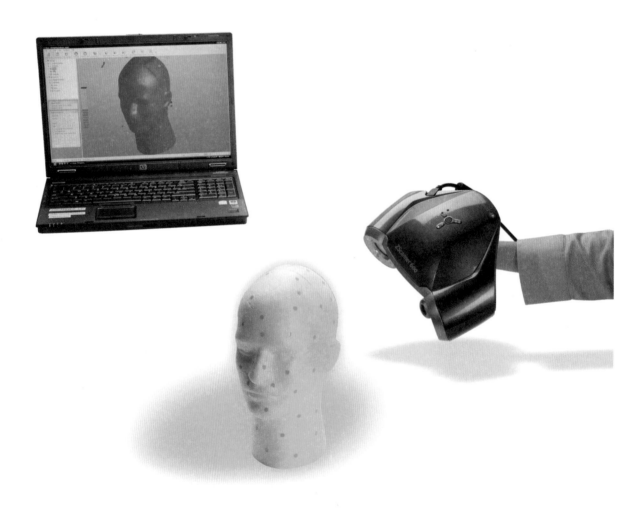

The hand-held ZScanner® 600 from Z Corporation allows automated continuous scanning without post-processing.

Raw data such as point clouds can be very difficult to work with, which is why manufacturers tend to provide software that simplifies, and to a large extent automates, the work. The quality of the software provided with the scanner is important, as the process can be largely automated with good software. In order to align different scans and data, the scanned object is often fitted with circular scanning points that help the software triangulate patches.

Chapter 16 on modelling clay shows how hand-held scanning was an important aspect of creating 3D CAD file data for the Olme Spyder (page 140). This data was then in turn used to mill a full-size car model in foam. The workflow was as follows:

| Scan 1/4 scale model | Construct new 3D geometry | CNC full-scale model |

Scanning can also be used to make a modification to an existing part. In the following example, the battery door on a portable GPS was scanned in and then exported to a 3D CAD system, where the model was modified to include a mounting bracket for a bicycle handlebar. In order to do this the scanned-in model was first turned into a solid 3D CAD model in the NextEngine ScanStudio™ software. This model was then exported to SolidWorks®, where the extra features were added.

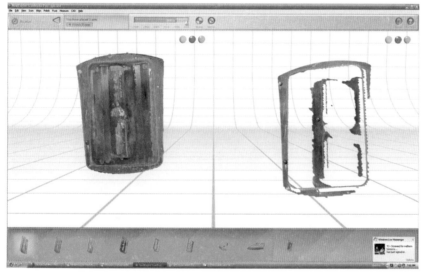

Portable GPS with new battery door containing a clip-on bracket for a bicycle handlebar.

The NextEngine ScanStudio™ software helped align different scans into a complete battery door and turned the meshes into a solid model. The scanned-in solid model was exported to SolidWorks®, where the snap-on feature for the handlebar clip was added.

The new battery door (white) was printed on a Dimension 3D printer, based on data scanned in from the original battery door (black).

TOOLS
Basic Hand Tools

Safety Check

— Read Chapter 5 on health and safety, pay particular attention to mechanical hazards, personal protective equipment and risk assessment
— Keep all your tools in good condition and use only for their intended purpose
— Store tools and materials away from children

Basic Toolset

It does not take an abundance of tools to start making models. A basic toolset will allow you to produce low-fidelity models in a variety of materials including paper, cardboard, foamboard and various types of foam. As shown in the Prototyping section of this book, these low-fidelity models precede the higher-fidelity models and are a big part of the design process. The basic toolkit includes simple hand tools, glues, fillers and personal protection equipment. It is a wise investment to start building this toolkit while in school, as it will serve you as a practising designer for years to come. Keep your tools in a suitable toolbox.

A good toolbox is essential for safely organizing and storing your personal tools. It typically contains items including: safety glasses, glue, filler, knives, measuring tools, small hobby saws, rasps, rotary tool and pliers.

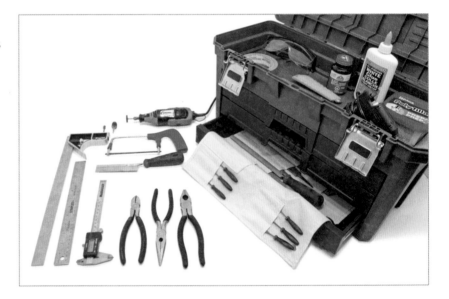

Layout and Measurement

Good workmanship starts with accuracy of measurement. The use of appropriate measuring tools is crucial to obtaining reasonable results. There are three basic measurement tools that need to form part of any designer's toolkit: a steel rule, a vernier caliper and a steel square.

The steel rule is used to mark straight lines or to guide cuts with a Stanley knife or scalpel. The steel rule can be used to measure overall dimensions to an accuracy of half a millimetre at best, which is why a set of electronic vernier calipers are used for dimensional accuracy instead. The caliper measures thickness, depth and width to an accuracy of one hundredth (0.01) of a millimetre (0.0004in). Steel squares are used to mark a perpendicular line to an edge of material. They are also used to create a vertical line when standing on the adjustable base.

Steel rule (top), steel square with adjustable base (middle), electronic vernier caliper (bottom).

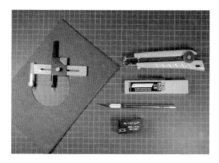

A Stanley knife and scalpel should be stocked with extra blades and used on a cutting mat.

Rasps have large teeth and are essential for rough shaping of wood and other soft materials.

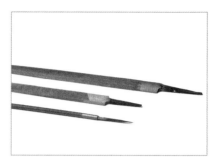

It is useful to have both flat and round files available.

Needle files are sold in kits and are for fine work and detail.

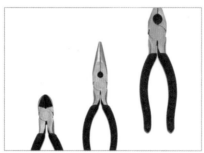

Pliers come in many shapes and sizes, including diagonal, long nose and combination types.

Different grit sandpapers are required for modelmaking. A basic toolset includes a range of coarse to fine sandpaper.

Cutting Tools

Precision-cutting tools include the scalpel and the Stanley knife. These should be stocked with an ample supply of sharp replacement blades. Make sure not to leave knife blades exposed and to keep all knives and blades safely away from children. Also wear eye protection, since a snapped blade creates a potential hazard. A cutting mat is essential for safety and will extend the life of the cutting blades, protect furniture and create a better and cleaner cut. Specialty cutters such as the circle cutter or a mitre cutter are not essential, but can save time.

Files and Rasps

Hand-shaping various materials requires a good set of rasps and files. Rasps will work effectively at removing large amounts of material from wood or foam. Files also work on a variety of materials and are useful for removing burrs and sharp edges on metal and plastic sheet. A workflow using rasps is shown in Chapter 15 (page 135). These tools are always used in conjunction with a vice to secure the workpiece.

Assortment of Other Small Modelmaking Tools

Other small hand-held tools include a hobby saw as well as pliers to hold small pieces while gluing and also to bend or cut small pieces of metal or wire.

Sandpaper

Sandpaper varies in coarseness, or grit. The lower the grit number, the coarser the paper. Sandpaper with grit below 100 is very coarse and will remove material quickly and can therefore be used to shape a surface. The medium-grit sandpaper of 240–320 will create a fairly smooth finish, whereas grit of 400–600 will start to polish the part. Different grits are therefore used in succession.

Power Tools and Machine Shop Tools

Rotary tools, such as this one made by Dremel, include a wide array of small bits suited to modelmaking work.

Hand-held drill, circular saw and jigsaw.

Table-mounted and floor-standing drill presses.

Drill press speed can be adjusted through a pulley arrangement between the motor and spindle. This should only be done when the machine is stopped and unplugged. The chart on the bottom of the guard cover on this machine shows speed options.

Safety Check

— Read Chapter 5 on health and safety, pay particular attention to mechanical hazards, personal protective equipment and risk assessment
— Keep all your tools in good condition and use only for their intended purpose
— Store tools and materials away from children

Workshop tools can loosely be categorized into three categories. Hand-held power tools are quite common and are sold for professional as well as home use. Stationary power tools include hobbyist varieties. The last category consists of larger industrial machine tools. Never operate any power or machine tool without obtaining professional training and supervision. The following description of various power tools is simply an overview of what they are used for and should in no way be interpreted as a substitute for proper training and education in the use of these tools. As a general safety preparation:

— Always wear safety glasses when using power tools
— Tie back long hair and remove loose clothing and jewellery that could become caught in the machine
— Wear proper footwear

Hand-Held Power Tools

A rotary hobby tool is a versatile modelmaking tool. It is supplied with a number of tool bits for cutting and grinding, as well as sanding. They are a useful addition to most basic toolkits, given their small size and versatility. Dremel is a popular brand of these tools.

Larger hand-held power tools include a cordless drill, a circular saw for cutting sheet materials and a jigsaw for cutting more complex outlines in sheet materials. Cordless versions now exist of many of these types of tools, adding even more mobility and flexibility.

Stationary Power Tools

Drill Press
The drill press (or pillar drill) is more accurate than a hand-held power drill and will provide more guidance and control during the drilling operation. Drill presses can also be used with circular saws, drum sanders and countersinks. The drill press is either floor or bench mounted and has an adjustable table that can be lowered or raised depending on the size of the workpiece. The drill bits are mounted in a chuck that turns via a motor. The speed can be changed through a pulley arrangement on top of the machine, which should only be adjusted when the machine has stopped and is unplugged.

Different materials require different cutting speeds. Steel, for example, needs to be cut at a slower speed than aluminium and also requires that cutting oil be used. A smaller diameter tool also requires a higher speed than a large diameter tool, since the velocity at the tool perimeter is lower. Refer to a drill speed chart for recommended speeds.

In addition to the general safety preparations listed above:

— Do not operate a drill press without adequate training and supervision
— Never hold a workpiece by hand, instead secure it by clamping it solidly to the work table
— Tie back long hair and remove loose clothing and jewellery that could become caught in the machine
— When drilling large pieces, secure them on the left side of the work bed as an extra safety precaution. A dislodged piece will then hit the back column
— Do not wear gloves that can become caught in the rotating spindle
— Never try to stop the drill by hand
— Unplug the machine before changing speeds
— Remove chuck key before starting the machine

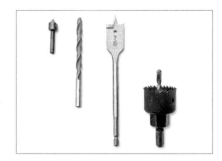

Different types of drill bits from left to right; countersink, twistdrill, spade drill and holesaw.

Bandsaw

This is one of the most versatile power tools for modelmaking purposes. It can be used to cut a variety of materials, including plastics, polystyrene foam, polyurethane modelling board, wood and metals. A 36cm (14in) bandsaw is a standard feature in many small workshops. The bandsaw blade is tensioned between two wheels that rotate it in a circular path. A saw-blade guide has to be adjusted to be almost flush with the top of the workpiece, before cutting.

The bandsaw can be used to make straight or angled cuts, as well as curved cuts. This power saw can do the jobs of most other saws put together. A thin blade will allow the bandsaw to work like a jigsaw and cut the most intricate detail, whereas a thick blade will allow for a straight-line cut much like a table saw.

In addition to the general safety preparations listed above:

The bandsaw is a versatile shop tool for sawing straight as well as being useful for contoured cuts.

— Do not operate the bandsaw without adequate training and supervision
— Always keep your fingers and hands away from the path of the blade in case you slip
— Make sure that safety guards are in place and that the vertical guide/guard is adjusted to an appropriate height above the workpiece
— Use a push stick to push material through saw
— Never change blades without stopping and disconnecting power to machine

Scroll saw

The scroll saw is similar to the table saw and is one of the more versatile power tools for modelmaking. The scroll saw has the benefit of being able to create an internal opening. Since the saw blade is removable it can be inserted into a hole opening to create the cut from inside. If a scroll saw is not available, a hand-held jigsaw can usually be used. Scroll saws have an upward and downward stroke that tends to pull the workpiece vertically. It is therefore important to maintain a good grip on the workpiece. This involves both using the machine's hold-down foot and maintaining sufficient manual pressure on top of the workpiece.

The scroll saw produces intricate contoured cuts

In addition to the general safety preparations listed above:

— Do not operate the scroll saw without adequate training and supervision
— Always keep your fingers and hands away from the path of the blade in case you slip
— Use the hold-down device and sufficient pressure to keep workpiece secure
— Never change blades without disconnecting power to machine

Sanding Disc, Belt and Post Sanders

Stationary belt sanders are useful for flattening and creating curves or for sculpting surfaces. The disc sander operates in much the same way, but is more suitable for fine detail work and fitting. Smaller desktop machines are usually combined into one unit. Belt and disc sanders are usually used after the bandsaw to create the final edge finish. The outline is cut using a template, leaving approximately 1–2mm (1/16 in) extra for sanding.

The post sander is a useful tool for sanding cavities and concave shapes. It can also be used to shape circular openings after scroll sawing. For the small workshop, this tool can be substituted with a drum sander fitted on to a drill press.

In addition to the general safety preparations listed above:

— Do not operate power sanders without adequate training and supervision
— Make sure to have a dust-collection system running and wear a dust mask
— Always keep your fingers and hands away from the sanding surfaces
— The clearance between the sanding surface and work table should be adjusted to be minimal to prevent material from being pulled into the crack

Disc sander (top) and small desktop belt sander (above).

A post sander creates concave curves in various diameters (right, above). A drill press can be fitted with drum sander attachments for lighter work (right).

Machine Tools

These machines are generally found in large machine shops as well as many schools, but require an exceptionally high level of training and supervision. When used in a safe, professionally supervised situation, then manual machine tools are still very useful as they produce very accurate parts. The cutting speeds and feeds have to be controlled and are a function of the material and cutting operation. Material is not removed in one pass, instead it is taken off in steps involving rough and final finishing cuts. A rough cut involves removing a larger amount of material than the final cut, but does not have the same fine finish.

Lathe

Woodworking lathes and metalworking lathes are two different types of machine that operate on the same principle. The workpiece is rotated, also known as turned, against a cutting tool that removes material to create radial symmetry, for example, bowls or cylindrical and conical shapes. The size of a part is limited to the maximum diameter that can be swung above the bed while turning. This is a function of the clearance between the bed and the revolving headstock spindle. The workpiece can be mounted directly onto a faceplate, held in a chuck or between the two mounting ends. Proper set-up and mounting is highly dependent on the shape of the part and the operation. It is therefore very important to get a technician to advise and guide you through the steps.

In the woodworking lathe, the cutting tools are held and guided by hand. This means that the accuracy is dependent on skill. Material is removed gradually and in steps. Templates are usually used to check the form, but only while the machine is turned off and the spindle has stopped turning. There are a wide variety of cutting tools that are suitable for different types of cut and detail. The basic tools include gouges for material removal, chisels for detailing and parting tools to cut deep grooves or to separate the part.

The metal-cutting lathe is a much more complicated piece of machinery. The cutting tools are guided and held in a carriage that can be accurately positioned using a hand wheel or a power leadscrew. This is a precision tool where all measurements are calculated and measured using the dials and settings on the machine. Metal-cutting lathes are also used to machine screw-threads. Specific tools are used for roughing cuts and for finishing cuts. The cutting tools are also specific to the material being turned.

Please see the safety reminder at the end of this section as well.

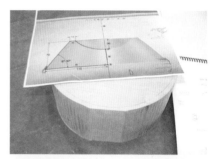

A wood instructor supervises a student using a wood-turning lathe.

This bowl-shaped vacuum-forming mould was made on the wood-turning mill using a computer-generated template as a guide.

The metalworking lathe is a high-precision machine that moves the cutter along three axes to cut circular items. In this case the brass workpiece is held in a 3-jaw chuck. A clear polycarbonate guard is folded down during the machining.

A knee mill can be used to create a variety of accurate cuts.

The Vertical Mill

The vertical mill resembles a drill press, except that it has three axes that allow the operator accurately to move a cutting tool relative to a fixed workpiece while cutting. Smaller desktop mills simply have a movable XY table, whereas larger knee mills allow the table to be raised and lowered as well, to accommodate larger workpieces. The accuracy of the movement is based on manual or electronic indicators. The head on the mill can be swivelled to perform angled cuts. A rotary axis can be added to machine circular shapes with a mill (similar to turning).

The end mill is the standard cutting tool for the milling machine and is available in two- or four-flute designs. End mills come in different diameters and lengths, suitable for a variety of cutting operations. The end mill can be used to mill holes, slots, pockets and surface cuts. For example, a pocket can be milled by lowering the end mill into the material and then tracing the contour of the pocket.

Machine tools are very complicated and involve a high level of understanding of materials, fixturing and set-up, as well as tool selection and machine setting. Machine shop technicians go to school and study this subject in detail, followed by significant industry training. It is paramount to understand that whereas this equipment is useful and a valuable teaching tool, these are dangerous and powerful tools that can easily cause very serious harm or death if treated casually or without proper training and supervision.

In addition to the general safety measures listed in this book:

— Do not operate any machine without adequate training and supervision
— Never attempt a set-up or operation that you have not been trained to do
— Know exactly where the emergency stop and off switches are located
— Make sure all safety guards are properly in place
— Always wear safety glasses
— Tie back long hair. Remove loose clothing and jewellery that could become caught in the machine. Do not wear gloves
— Never touch or try to remove shavings by hand while the machine is running
— Never reach around or behind the workpiece, nor attempt to do any measurements while the machine is running

A slot is milled in high-density polyurethane modelling board using a two-flute end-mill cutter.

Rapid Prototyping

Safety Check

— Read Chapter 5 on health and safety
— Obtain SDS for any uncured rapid prototyping materials that you handle or for any materials used for infiltration

Rapid prototyping (RP) is an additive computer-controlled process that builds parts inside a machine, layer by layer, using a variety of materials and processes. Also known as solid free-form fabrication, additive manufacturing, or 3D printing, this technology has revolutionized modelmaking by enabling physical prototypes to be output directly from the computer. From its beginnings in the late 1980s to the present, it has transformed our thinking about making prototypes, changing the process from one that takes place in the confines of the workshop to one that requires no more complexity than sending a file to the printer. This ability has greatly affected the speed of product development. The complexity and detail inherent in rapid-prototyped parts is especially useful when creating models of injection-moulded plastic parts. Thin walls, bosses and ribs are difficult to make by any other method. It also means that the risk associated with making expensive and complicated mass-production tooling is reduced, since the design can be evaluated and tested for form, fit and function prior to tooling.

There are both advantages and limitations inherent in rapid prototyping:

Such parts as these can be printed in a matter of hours, allowing students to incorporate more detail into their projects.

Advantages
— Parts can have complex geometry (for example, all the typical internal features seen in an injection-moulded part) making them very useful for part verification prior to tooling
— Cleaner and safer compared to traditional machine shop practice
— Encourages more iteration
— Easier to make hollow parts that can be fitted with electronic or mechanical components

Limitations
— Material choices
— Requires access to a 3D CAD system
— Size of build volume
— Cost is directly related to volume
— Simulates predominantly plastics, rather than other materials such as textiles

Process

The development of rapid prototyping is tied directly to the development of 3D solid computer modelling, which made it possible to fully describe a solid object on the computer. It is necessary to have access to a 3D CAD program, and the required skill therefore moves from being able to build the parts physically to being able to manipulate 3D geometry on the computer. This fact is often overlooked, and the efficacy of the process can be severely affected if the designer does not have a good grasp of 3D CAD. The type of software used also affects the process. Parametric solid modelling software programs, such as Creo™ Elements/Pro™, SolidWorks® or Autodesk Inventor®, are inherently solid-based, whereas some software is primarily surface-based and requires that the operator knows how to stitch all the different surfaces together to describe a watertight solid that in turn can be printed. Once the 3D CAD geometry has been created as a solid, it is possible to create a rapid prototyping part.

The resolution of an STL file is a function of a number of triangles that approximate the shape. The file on the bottom is three times larger than the one on top, but would create a smoother surface.

CatalystEX software is used to prepare a part for printing on a Dimension 3D printer. The software creates support structure automatically.

Data Translation

The 3D CAD file must first be translated into a format that the rapid prototyping system can read. This is known as an STL (stereolithography) file format and comes pre-packaged with most of the typical software programs used for CAD. The STL file is simply an approximation of the original solid using a triangulated surface mesh that is easy to import and manipulate in the rapid prototyping system. It is important to set the tessellation quality to be appropriate to the surface being generated. A sphere, for example, will require more triangles than a flat plane.

Rapid prototyping software then creates a series of sections, or slices, taken vertically through the model. These sections will be used to produce the 3D model. Each slice must be described as an enclosed area, which is printed sequentially one layer on top of the next until the entire volume has been created.

The software also has to determine if there are areas where a section is unsupported during the printing cycle. This happens when the geometry is overhanging or otherwise unsupported from below. The rapid prototyping systems therefore need some way in which to add support structure during the printing process in order to prevent the model collapsing while being built. Part orientation during the build is a major consideration since it affects how much support structure is required.

Technology Considerations

There are many differences between the various rapid prototyping technologies. The following overview of the fundamental technologies and systems is not meant to pinpoint specifications, since they continue to evolve and improve. It does, however, highlight some of the inherent advantages and limitations of various systems. It is worth considering many different issues when selecting a process for prototyping as in most cases it is a matter of trade-off between cost, speed and material properties.

What is the Difference between Industrial RP Systems and 3D Printers?

When rapid prototyping (RP) systems first emerged in the late 1980s, the high cost and complexity confined them to service bureaus or large corporations with dedicated prototyping facilities. At that time 3D solid modelling software was also expensive and less common than 2D drafting programs. The next ten years saw a drastic reduction in cost of solid modelling software and as it started to become the norm, the demand for rapid prototyping parts grew substantially. New RP technologies started to emerge to tap into this larger market. Consequently, the cost, size and complexity of rapid prototyping equipment dropped significantly, to the point that schools and design offices can now afford to own and operate their own machines. The smaller systems are generally referred to as 3D printers and are intended to be easy to use and networked in an office environment. Whereas the industrial systems have tended to have larger build volumes, more material selection and better resolution than their 3D printing counterparts, there is rapid convergence in terms of these qualities that keeps making 3D printing ever more accessible and desktop-friendly. There are some limits though – at the time of writing the 3D printer systems offer very limited elastomeric or clear plastic part capability, although this is possible with higher-end systems. 3D printers can, however, be used to print a 3D pattern in order to make silicone moulds (see Chapter 17, page 147) from which clear or flexible prototype parts can be produced, although this does require extra work.

Some industrial systems are now starting to compete with mass-production technologies such as injection moulding. The resulting benefit is greater manufacturing flexibility since no tooling is required. Tool-free production means you have the freedom to make changes more easily, get up and running faster and not have to worry about sink marks, draft angles and a host of other injection-moulding issues associated with steel tooling. The onus on the industrial systems is therefore to reduce post-operative procedures, while increasing accuracy and throughput in order to be competitive.

Build Material

The RP systems are classified according to the different material technologies they use: photo-curable liquids (photopolymers), solid powders or extruded plastic. The material selection is an important aspect of prototyping. The range of material properties needs to be considered carefully in the prototyping process, as there are associated trade-offs in cost, strength, surface quality and colour. If it is a works-like prototype that is to be handled and subjected to loads, it will need to have more strength than if it is a looks-like prototype made mostly for show and tell. The looks-like prototype on the other hand will need a high-level cosmetic finish if it is to be used for trade shows or other promotional material, such as pictures for packaging. This level of prototype may instead require a material and process that provides a better surface finish. Another trade-off is that many photopolymers are sensitive to heat and may deflect, or deform, even at modestly elevated temperatures. The heat deflection temperature (HDT) data therefore should be examined to see if it is applicable to the prototyping application.

For interactive electronic products, rapid prototypes are perfect because electronic components can easily be incorporated. For casings that are meant to be repeatedly assembled and disassembled, it is advisable to use threaded brass parts that are typically inserted into plastic bosses using a soldering iron. They can also be glued into oversized holes with cyanoacrylate glue (see page 79).

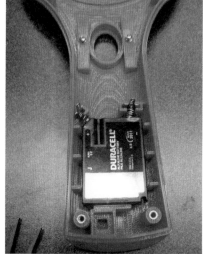

Rapid prototype parts can be fitted with threaded brass inserts. These allow easier opening and closing of the housing using machine screws.

Layer Thickness: The Staircase Effect

The surface quality of the parts is dictated by how thick the individual print layers are. The surface will be approximated by a series of parallel cross sections, so the thinner these are the closer they will replicate the surface smoothness. The effect is more visible on curved surfaces and is called a staircase effect. A finer staircase is possible by building thinner layers at a time – something that can vary significantly among different systems. Orientation of the part during the build cycle is also important as it can greatly affect the surface quality of the part. A cylinder built vertically will have smooth sides, whereas if built on its side it will need support and have substantial staircasing.

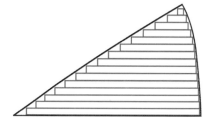

The staircase effect is more visible on a gradually curved surface and with systems that use thicker build layers.

Post-Processing

Post-processing includes everything that needs to be done to the part after it is removed from the prototyping machine. This can include removal of support structures, material curing or infusion of strengthening materials. In each case the function of the prototype's intended purpose must be considered. Staircasing may need to be removed for cosmetic prototypes, requiring extra filling and sanding of the parts prior to painting. Conversely, this may not be necessary for functional prototypes made for verification, where accuracy and strength may instead be more important.

Build Size

The maximum build size is usually described in XYZ coordinates. The 3D printing systems are generally capable of smaller parts than their industrial equivalents.

Larger parts can be made with some planning by splitting the file into parts, which are then printed separately and joined together after printing. Given the fairly high cost of the materials, this is often where it becomes important to consider less expensive modelmaking routes that involve an approach other than rapid prototyping.

Material Cost

There is generally a trade-off between cost, surface quality and material strength. Less expensive materials might be suitable for certain applications where appearance rather than strength or flexibility is of importance. The cost can be a significant issue if the model is large. The cost of the material also needs to be considered in terms of cost of support structure material (typically a secondary material) and any secondary processing, such as secondary material infusion for strength.

Level of Finish

There is both time and cost associated with the manual labour involved in finishing parts. This again is highly dependent on the purpose of the prototype. If the model is made simply to test fit and function, very little or no finishing is necessary. The most time-consuming models tend to be the high-fidelity appearance models used for communication. This is where it makes sense to have the best possible surface quality to begin with.

Service bureaus tend to offer various levels of finishing. The basic level tends simply to include removing the support structures and perhaps bead-blasting the parts. A higher level of finish might include manual sanding to remove staircasing. A still higher level might include further sanding and primer ready for paint. If required, the service bureaus will completely finish the parts to any level of production quality appearance, including high-quality surface paint or electroplating.

Students can accomplish very high-quality results by using fillers and paint: water-based products are usually the safer option. Chapter 18 on painting (page 154) shows how to finish a rapid prototype similar to those below to a smooth glossy finish, such as this painted metallic finish (using water-based products).

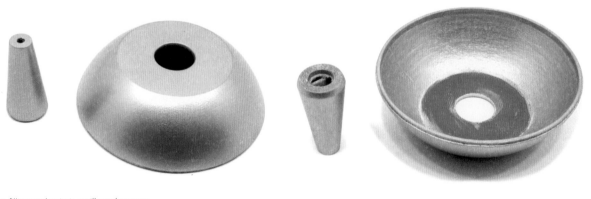

Sanding, filling and painting will produce very good cosmetic surfaces, as shown on the left. The inside of the part on the right shows what it would look like if painted without extra preparation.

Powder-Based Technology

These types of system use a powder-based substrate that is deposited in thin additive layers and then hardened only in the area defined by the part's cross section. The extra powder surrounding the parts presents some inherent advantages. First of all it serves as a natural support structure. Secondly, the extra powder is simply reused, thereby minimizing material usage. The powder also allows parts to be nested easily, without the need for more complex support structures to bridge the parts. Powder-based materials are used in industrial as well as desktop 3D printer systems, but the process and materials used in the two systems shown in this book differ markedly from each other.

Industrial System – Selective Laser Sintering (SLS)

Selective Laser Sintering (SLS) is a rapid prototyping technology sold by 3D Systems Corporation, South Carolina. The technology has been around since the early 1990s and is therefore one of the pioneering methods of rapid prototyping. These industrial RP systems will produce parts in a wide range of materials that are selectively sintered with a laser. It works by depositing a thin layer of powder material in a build chamber, which is then selectively sintered (fused with heat) from a CO_2 laser. The process is continued layer by layer until the part is complete. The materials include a variety of consumer- and engineering-grade plastics: polypropylene for living hinges, glass-reinforced plastics for strength, and elastomeric materials to produce anything from shoe soles to gaskets. SLS also produces durable plastic and metal parts through direct laser sintering that are also suitable for end use applications.

3D Printer – Z Corporation

Z Corporation has offered powder-based 3D printing since the mid-1990s. The basis of its technology is the use of consumer inkjet printing on top of a layer of plaster powder. As the inkjet prints the cross section it applies a binder that holds the printed area together. This is repeated in fine increments, by automatically lowering the build volume and applying a new fine layer of plaster. Thanks to a multiple printhead approach, each layer prints very quickly, allowing a high vertical build speed. Containment of the fine powder is a consideration, since parts need to be physically removed from the powder tray and cleaned of excess powder.

   As the printers increase in size and cost, they also tend to offer a higher throughput, better accuracy and more colours.

The sPro 240 Selective Laser Sintering machine is used to create parts in a range of consumer and engineering grade materials.

The accuracy and strength of this SLS prototype for the Motion Computing J3400 tablet allowed mechanical testing at the critical stage of design and engineering implementation.

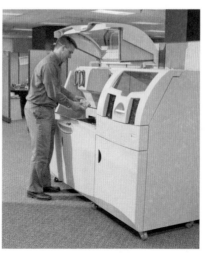

Z Corporation's entry-level ZPrinter® 150 (far left) and largest ZPrinter® 650 (left) both use plaster powder and inkjet technology to produce parts quickly and cost-effectively.

ZPrinter® parts can be produced in a full range of colours. Shown are Reebok DMX shoe soles (right) and Sea-Doo® Seascooter™ underwater propulsion system (below) prototypes printed on a ZPrinter®.

The simple and low-cost material is excellent for conceptual modelmaking, but the strength of the parts as printed is somewhat limited in functional applications. The strength can, however, be increased through post-processing. Plaster parts have minute air pockets that can be infiltrated with secondary materials to provide added strength. Salt water, wax, cyanoacrylate glue (super glue) or two-part epoxy can be used for plaster infiltration. Z Corporation produces three different infiltrants. Water Clear is a saltwater-based infusion system that models are dipped into. For stronger and more functional prototypes the Z-Bond cyanoacrylate infiltrant has been developed, and for even more structural applications Z-Max epoxy-based infiltrant is used.

The printed part is removed from plaster build tray.

Parts are infused with salt water, cyanoacrylate or two-part epoxy depending on the intended use and application.

Solid-Based Technology

The predominant solid-based technology is known as fused deposition modelling (FDM), a process developed and patented by Stratasys Inc. This process works by feeding a thin filament of ABS into a heated extrusion head. FDM is available both as high-end industrial machines and smaller 3D printer systems.

Industrial – Fortus

The Fortus™ range of FDM equipment from Stratasys can produce large structural parts even for small-scale manufacturing or industrial fixtures. Parts can be made in ABS, polycarbonate or Ultem engineering-grade plastic.

3D Printer – Dimension uPrint

Stratasys also produces the Dimension uPrint® range of 3D printers (known as HP Designjet 3D printers in Europe) for in-house prototyping. These are extremely easy to use as the materials are held in print cartridges, which can be replaced on the fly to change colour or add material. There is a separate cartridge for the material used for the support structure.

Depending on the machine model, the support structure is either an easy breakaway material or a water-soluble material. The water-soluble type of structure is more suitable for thin-walled and delicate parts that may be damaged in the breakaway process.

Support structures are either washed away in a special water-based solution or simply peeled away in the case of the breakaway system.

The Fortus 900mc from Stratasys is an industrial 3D production system capable of producing parts in a variety of engineering-grade plastics.

Lawnmower prototype made by Fortus™ FDM.

Small-scale production of parts in real plastics saves money on injection-mould tooling.

Dimension 3D printers use real ABS plastic to create parts.

ABS material spool cartridge loaded into the 3D printer. A similar cartridge exists for the support structure material.

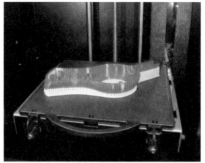

Extrusion printhead traces the outline of the part (in red) while also building a breakaway support structure (grey).

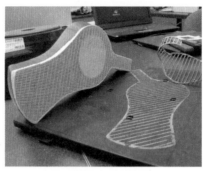

The part is removed from the platen with a steel scraper and the breakaway support structure is then manually peeled off.

For functional and verificational prototypes the parts do not usually need additional finishing. For visually cosmetic parts it is necessary both to sand and to fill the exterior surfaces prior to painting.

Liquid-Based Systems

Liquid-based systems use photopolymers that are cured with an ultraviolet light source. These can produce very fine layer thicknesses that in turn have very good surface quality requiring little or no extra finishing. The heat deflection temperature for some of the materials is quite low and should be considered.

Stereolithography machines from 3D Systems, such as this SLA7000, produce parts from laser-cured photopolymers.

Industrial System – 3D Systems' Stereolithography Apparatus (SLA)

The first additive rapid prototyping technology was the Stereolithography Apparatus (SLA). It was invented in 1986 by South Carolina-based 3D Systems Corporation and commercialized in 1988, along with the STL file format. SLA is characterized by high surface quality and smoothness of the parts.

    The technology makes use of a UV laser that is directed on to the surface of a vat of photopolymer. The laser traces the slices of the STL (stereolithography) files on to the surface of the liquid, which is then locally cured by the energy from the laser. The hardened section can be lowered and recoated with photopolymer so that the next section can be created. This process continues until the entire part has been created. Support structures are generated during the build to support overhangs and voids within the object. After printing, the support structure is removed. The smooth surface quality and fine feature detail is a function of the fine layer thickness. 3D Systems' Viper™ SLA system, for example, builds at a mere 0.02mm layer thickness, eliminating most staircasing. There is a wide range of materials available for this process that mimic the material properties of some common plastic production materials. The larger industrial systems such as the iPro® 9000 XL SLA system will produce parts as large as 1499 x 762 x 508mm (59 x 30 x 20in).

Large, accurate SLAs are commonly used to verify part design prior to tooling production.

Office 3D Printer – Objet Geometries

Objet Geometries produces a series of desktop 3D printing systems using acrylic-based photopolymers that are cured instantly with UV light. These systems also produce very smooth high-quality parts.

 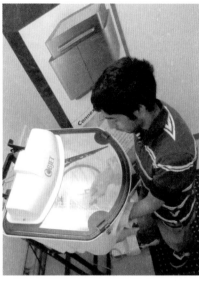

The Objet30 3D printer from Objet Geometries produces acrylic parts made from UV-cured photopolymers. The support system is cleaned off in a wash station (left).

Objet's FullCure® Materials range is composed of rigid materials with strength characteristics that simulate ABS as well as polypropylene. There are also rubber-like materials that simulate the properties of thermoplastic elastomers or silicone. The PolyJet™ technology uses dual printheads to print modelling and support material simultaneously. The parts require no post-curing, but the support material has to be washed off. Objet parts are characterized by extremely thin build layers producing high-quality surface parts. The Objet24 and Objet30 printers are the entry-level systems and produce parts in very fine build layers of 0.028mm. They are currently limited to printing rigid opaque type materials. The higher-end Eden350V™ printer produces even finer surface quality using layers of 0.016mm, and prints the entire range of materials including optically clear parts. At the very high end, Objet's Connex family of printers uses PolyJet Matrix™ technology, which can print multiple model materials simultaneously to create what the company terms composite Digital Materials™. This also allows the machine to simulate plastic injection moulding of parts with overmoulded elastomeric sections.

The Connex family of 3D printers from Objet Geometries can produce multiple parts, such as the overmoulded elastomeric wheel below.

Summary

Desktop 3D printers have become very good and produce accurate parts that can be used for a variety of prototyping needs. The industrial-type rapid prototyping and desktop 3D printer systems continue to converge in terms of quality of parts and material offerings. The high-end industrial systems will continue to offer larger parts and more throughput, making them a reasonable alternative to injection moulding for many small- to medium-scale production runs.

CNC Machining and Laser Cutting

Safety Check

— Read Chapter 5 on health and safety, pay particular attention to mechanical hazards, personal protective equipment and risk assessment
— Read SDS for materials before cutting
— Obtain professional training and supervision before using CNC or laser-cutting equipment

Whereas the term rapid prototyping has mostly become synonymous with additive digital prototyping processes, there are also subtractive digital prototyping methods that remove material from a solid block or sheet of material in a rapid fashion. Computer Numerical Control (CNC) is a term that refers to computer-guided machining. This part of the chapter will focus on CNC milling machines and laser cutters, both of which are commonly used in modelmaking. These tools add a level of detail, speed and precision that saves a great deal of time for high-fidelity prototyping.

CNC Machining

CNC machining is a subtractive process using milling-cutter tools to remove material. It starts with a solid chunk of material, which is carved away until the final shape is achieved. Compared to traditional and manual machining it offers many benefits, most notably the ability to produce very complex surface geometry from computer files. Some of the uses for CNC prototype milling include:

— Vacuum-forming tools (see Chapter 13, page 116).
— Sculptural forms in a variety of materials (see polystyrene foam, polyurethane modelling board and wood in Chapters 12, 14 and 15)
— Moulds for making silicone flexible parts (see Chapter 17, page 147)

Milling can be a complex and specialized skill and requires professional training and supervision. The purpose of this part of the chapter is solely to describe the basic technology of CNC machining and is not meant for training.

Advantages
— Material selection is very broad and includes plastic, metals, foams, modelling board and wood
— Material cost can be much less than that of rapid prototyping
— Surface quality can be extremely high
— Precision is extremely high
— Not as stringent a need for 3D solids modelling, since 3D surface data can be used

Limitations
— Requires special training
— Requires knowledge of fixturing
— Requires knowledge of Computer Aided Manufacturing software (note: this varies from very simple to very complex)
— Fine features require very fine cutters

Large industrial CNC machining centres are suitable for reproducing duplicate detailed parts in metal, such as the aluminium housing on the left.

— Overhangs can present a problem when the underside cannot be reached by a tool. This may require more than three-axis machining or multiple set-ups
— Subtractive modelling can create dust or shavings

CNC machines are an outgrowth of traditional milling machine technology. They translate a workpiece along different axes relative to a cutter that removes material. The most common is a three-axis machine, that allows the cutting tool to be positioned relative to the cutting surface at any point defined by X, Y and Z coordinates.

Industrial CNC Milling Centres

At the high end of the spectrum are the CNC machining centres. These are heavy industrial machines primarily developed to cut metals. Tool changers allow the machine selectively to perform different types of machining operations, including milling, drilling and tapping. These production machines are intended to produce many identical parts to close tolerances and specifications. The high cost, large footprint and power requirements restrict this type of equipment to industrial environments.

Desktop CNC Mills

Smaller machines have been developed to cater to the woodworker or hobbyist. These types of machine work well with such materials as wood, plastics and polyurethane modelling board. Since many models are built from those materials, they are also suitable machines for modelmaking. Ease of operation, small footprint and safety enclosures are incorporated to make it easier to use these types of machine in schools or a smaller workshop setting. Machines such as the Roland MDX-540 have been developed specifically to offer ease of use and safety. It is also available with a tool changer and an optional fourth axis.

CNC Routers

The CNC router is a large-footprint machine primarily developed for woodworking. These machines tend to have much larger X and Y ranges than Z ranges, since they are primarily used for cutting outlines. The cutting head is usually a high-speed router fitted with end-mill tooling. These are generally described as gantry-type machines, where the frame moves on top of the sheet material in all three axes.

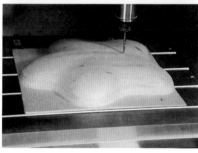

Desktop machines such as the Roland MDX-540 have been developed specifically to cater to a small workshop environment.

Wood routers are often used to cut outlines in sheet material, but some have a third axis to be able to control the vertical dimension.

A part is quickly machined in Styrofoam to check the tool path.

Tool Paths

The tool path is what guides the tool to create the surface of the part. These are created in Computer Aided Manufacturing (CAM) programs. These programs look like CAD programs and are increasingly sold as modules that work within programs such as Creo™ Elements/Pro™, SolidWorks® and Rhinoceros®. The tool paths are then sent from the CAM program to the CNC mill to create the part. Sometimes the paths are verified in softer materials such as polystyrene foam. This can save on costly mistakes.

The approach taken to machine prototypes is generally much simpler than the approach taken to machine production parts and can usually be broken down into two separate tool-path steps. The first tool path is used to create the rough cut. This is a time-saving step that removes a lot of material quickly and effectively without worrying about surface quality. The second tool path is used for the finishing cut.

This cut is performed with a small-diameter ball-nose end mill. The small diameter allows for a fine level of detail, such as creating tighter corners on inside radii or machining small holes or slots. The finishing cut will consist of a series of parallel cuts, where the tool essentially traces the entire surface of the part. In order to achieve a very high level of surface finish, the distance between the lines has to be kept very small. This is because the ball-nose cutter leaves a contour, known as a cusp height, which becomes flatter as the distance between the lines, or what is known as step-over, decreases. This greatly affects the machining time, which is why a high-quality surface takes orders of magnitude longer to machine than an approximate surface.

The first tool path is a rough cut. The second tool path is the finishing cut and takes longer.

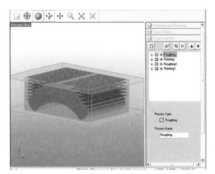 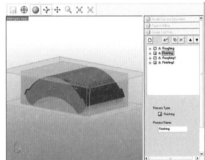

Surfaces are created by parallel tool paths as shown. When the cutter finishes a straight-line path, it steps over to begin the next path. Surface quality is a function of tool step-over. A smaller step-over creates a smoother finish, but takes longer to machine.

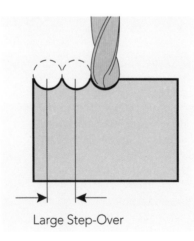 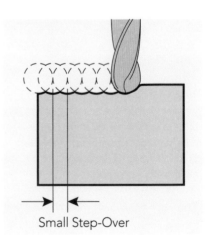

Large Step-Over   Small Step-Over

If the surface is very smooth without any fine details, then it may be possible to increase the size of the ball-nose cutter. This can actually both save time and improve the cutting quality, as the cusp height of the cut is smaller for a larger-diameter tool.

One-Sided versus Two-Sided Machining

A three-axis CNC mill can cut only from the top, which means there are no undercuts. In order to machine a part with undercuts, for example an egg, the part would need to be machined twice. If the inside is left solid, then the part can be split in two and joined together. This one-sided machining is fairly straightforward.

In order to make a thin-walled part, things get more complicated, since both sides of the same part need to be machined. This requires that the first side be machined and the part then flipped around to machine the inside.

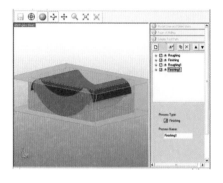
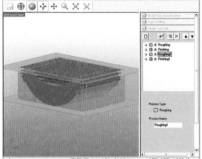

This shows how the bottom of the part would need new tool paths, for both roughing and finishing, in order to machine the entire part.

A fourth axis is a rotary axis that can rotate the workpiece automatically in order to machine multiple planes. If a fourth axis is used, then two-sided machining is usually quite simple, as the machine will rotate the part 180 degrees when the first side is done. Two-sided machining can, however, be accomplished with a three-axis machine. This requires that the workpiece be flipped manually and that two separate programs be created, one for the top and one for the bottom surface.

In both cases it is important to add physical supports to the part so that it does not become loose during the machining cycle. These are manually removed at the end.

Laser Cutting

Low-energy lasers are found in anything from laser pointers to printers, while higher-power devices can be used to burn or cut through materials. Laser cutting has been a very exciting new technology in both manufacturing and prototyping. The flexibility and speed of lasers is being used increasingly in sheet-metal work to create complex outlines for a variety of products. Whereas these industrial lasers are large and complex manufacturing systems, smaller CO_2 lasers that can be used to cut anything from plastic and paper sheet to wood are becoming more frequently utilized in schools. Furthermore, since they are limited to a two-dimensional outline (XY plane), it is possible to create the cutting geometry in a two-dimensional vector-based graphics program such as CorelDRAW® or Adobe Illustrator®. In Chapters 10 and 13 on paper and thermoplastic sheeting (pages 86 and 115), the process of laser cutting has been shown in the context of these materials. One important aspect to consider is that the machines require external ventilation to remove the gases created when material is burnt.

A thin-walled part machined on a three-axis machine. The top is machined and then the part is flipped over to machine the bottom. Note the two holes that are used for registration and the small amount of material that allows the part to hang on the frame.

Small CO2 lasers cut materials such as paper, plastic, fabric or wood.

Smaller CO2 lasers can also be used for engraving materials. Scanned-in pictures can be used to create motifs. Metals usually require a coating prior to the marking process.

A custom motif is laser-engraved on to a piece of wood in this student project.

Typical Small CO2 Laser Cutting Capabilities

Material	Laser Cutting	Laser Engraving
Acrylic	X	X
Styrene	Tends to melt	X
Paper and Card	X	X
Glass		X
Rubber Gasket Material	X	X
Ceramics		X
Wood Veneer	X	X
Anodized Aluminium		X
Bare Metal		Needs to be pre-coated with marking solution
It is important to check with manufacturers' technical specifications as capabilities vary with system and laser strength.		

ADHESIVES AND FILLERS

Safety Check

— Read Chapter 5 on health and safety, pay particular attention to hazardous substances and personal protective equipment
— Read material labels and SDS for glues and fillers
— Water-based products are usually safer alternatives
— Students should be aware of their school policy about materials

Glues

Modelmaking makes ample use of gluing as a form of assembly, as it is quicker and easier than most types of mechanical assembly. Gluing is also the basis for the additive modelling approach, where forms are assembled from their basic elements. Selecting the proper glue is a function of both application and material.

Typical Modelmaking Glues

Type of Glue	Typical Modelmaking Applications	Approximate Cure Time	Precautions*
Cyanoacrylate (Super Glue)	General modelmaking glue. Dissimilar materials can be joined.	Thin: 1–3 seconds Gap filling: 1–2 minutes	Bonds skin instantly; eye irritant: wear eye protection. Use in well-ventilated area.
Epoxy (two-part)	Where extra glue volume is needed. Dissimilar materials can be joined.	Set time varies from 5 minutes to 12 hours	Eye and skin irritant: wear gloves and eye protection. Use in well-ventilated area.
White Glue (PVA – Polyvinyl Acetate)	Paper, cardboard, polystyrene foam, foamboard, wood.	1 hour	May cause eye irritation, but is generally considered a safer glue.
Spray Glue	For joining sheet materials. Bonds to most materials.	30 seconds	Flammable and under pressure. Eye and skin irritant: wear eye protection. Use in well-ventilated area.
Glue Stick	Glue paper and paper templates on to other materials (non-permanent).	30 seconds	Normally considered a safer glue.
Hot Glue	For cardboard and foamboard mock-ups.	10–20 seconds	Can burn skin. Will melt polystyrene foam.
Rubber Cement	Glue paper and paper templates on to other materials (non-permanent).	10 seconds	Flammable. Eye and possible skin irritant: wear eye protection. Use in well-ventilated area.

* Also read each manufacturer's specific safety and use precautions and instructions as well as SDS.

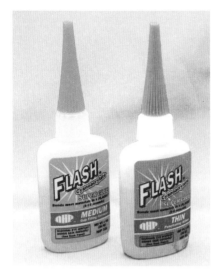

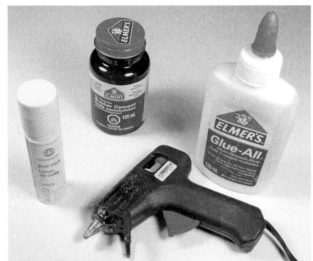

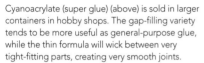

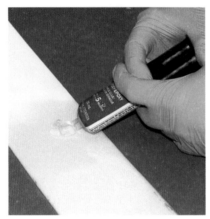

Cyanoacrylate (super glue) (above) is sold in larger containers in hobby shops. The gap-filling variety tends to be more useful as general-purpose glue, while the thin formula will wick between very tight-fitting parts, creating very smooth joints.

Glue sticks, rubber cement, white paper glue and hot glue (above centre) all work on paper. Spray glues (above right) should be used with extreme caution and in well-ventilated environments.

Epoxy two-part glues are available in many formulations and set times (right). A very strong glue for dissimilar materials but also creates more mess.

Tapes

Tapes are used for a variety of purposes. They are used for masking off areas during painting. They are used to hold parts together temporarily as well as permanently. Tapes are also used as guides for sanding or clay sculpting, as will be shown in Chapters 10 to 20 on materials. Drafting tape is a general-purpose tape for modelmaking that does not peel paper or leave glue residue on models: it is therefore preferable to masking tape. Double-sided tape is used to mount parts together both temporarily and permanently. It is also used for holding down softer materials during CNC machining or to stick sandpaper to sanding templates. There are many different grades of double-sided tape available as well as special-purpose varieties.

A selection of masking tapes (below left), and double-sided tape with protective backing on one side (below right). Drafting tape and low-tack plastic tape (below centre) are especially useful when masking on top of a painted surface, as they are less likely to peel the paint off.

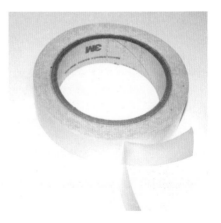

Fillers

Fillers have an important function in modelmaking. They fill in gaps that exist when two parts are joined together and can therefore be used to create a seamless part from separate elements. Fillers are used to create certain features, such as inside fillets. They are also used to fill scratches or to repair mistakes. Fillers need to be sanded smooth to the substrate. The filler should always be softer than the substrate. If the filler is harder then it is impossible to achieve a good finish, since the substrate will sand instead of the filler. They are either water- or organic solvent-soluble. Wear dust masks, and vacuum dust particles frequently with a fine-particle filter or use a dust-collection system.

Typical Modelmaking Fillers

Type of Filler	Typical Modelmaking Applications	Benefits	Precautions*
Automotive Body Filler	Thick fill areas and volume. Adheres to most materials. Do not use with Styrofoam.	Quick cure time. Feathers well.	Solvents are flammable and pose health risk. Use only in well-ventilated area. Wear gloves.
Automotive Spot Filler	Thick fill areas and volume. Adheres to most materials. Can be sculpted.	Sands very smooth.	Solvents are flammable and pose health risk. Use only in well-ventilated area. Wear gloves.
Apoxie® Sculpt (Water-Soluble)	Paper, cardboard, polystyrene foam, foamboard, wood.	More environmental than body filler. Water clean-up.	Takes a long time to dry. Use only in well-ventilated area. Wear gloves.
Polyfilla (Water-Soluble)	Fine scratch and finishing. Adheres to most materials. Use with Styrofoam.	Water clean-up.	Wet-sand if possible. Limit exposure to dust. Wear gloves.
Wood Filler (Water-Soluble Varieties)	Mostly for wood, test on other substrates.	Similar to polyfilla but harder. Water clean-up.	Wet-sand if possible. Limit exposure to dust. Wear gloves.
* Also read each manufacturer's specific safety and use precautions and instructions as well as SDS. Always wear dust mask and eye protection when sanding any filler. Always wear rubber gloves when handling any uncured fillers.			

Solvent-Based Fillers

Automotive fillers and spot putties are generally used to fill and repair dents and scratches in cars. They have long been used in modelmaking because they set quickly, feather well and are easy to sand. The downside is that they contain organic solvents that pose health risks. They should only be used with very good ventilation (outside or in a paint booth). Body filler is generally used to build up volume or to create a seamless joint between two parts. It consists of a filler material that is mixed thoroughly with a hardener. It will set in approximately 20 minutes, after which it can be sanded smooth. The spot filler is generally applied on top of the body filler in order to smooth the surface and fill minor surface imperfections. This material dries by solvent evaporation, after which it can be sanded. Limit your exposure to dust when sanding (see above).

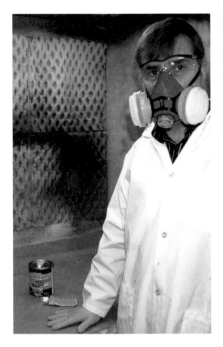

Mix solvent-based fillers in a well-ventilated area, a spray booth, outside or under a fume hood.

Automotive body filler is mixed according to the manufacturer's instructions. It is important to achieve a uniform colour consistency to ensure that mixing has been thorough.

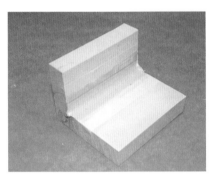

In making this inside corner, first body filler was used to build up the radius (left) and then a final layer of spot filler was used on top (middle) and sanded smooth (right).

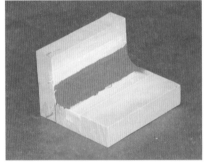

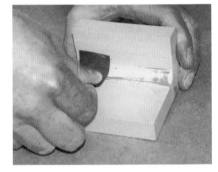

Pre-mixed water-based household polyfilla is a useful modelmaking filler and avoids solvents.

Water-Soluble Fillers

Water-based products are increasingly sought after, thanks to the easier clean-up and so as to avoid solvents. These materials should still be treated with caution, especially when sanding, as many fillers contain silica.

Household Polyfilla

Household polyfilla (or spackle) is found in hardware and DIY shops, as it has been developed as a general paint preparation material. Polyfilla is used to fill scratches and blemishes, and for filling smaller voids. Look for high-quality, non-shrinking pre-mixed varieties as shown on the left. These products can also be used to fill and finish 3D printer parts (see Chapter 18 on paint and finishing, page 159). Polyfilla does not have any structural strength, so it is only useful for cosmetic filling. Apply in thin layers and ideally place in front of a fan to allow it to dry rapidly.

General household polyfilla can be used as a substitute for automotive spot fillers, and does not have the same hazardous solvents. The lack of these solvents also allows polyfilla to be used on polystyrene foam, which would otherwise melt.

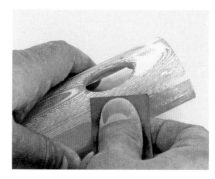

Water-Based Wood Filler

Water-based wood fillers are becoming more commonplace. They have been designed to fill larger cracks and voids. They can be used on other materials than just wood, but make sure to check compatibility on a piece of scrap material first. Drying time varies based on thickness. These are used just like polyfilla, but are more structural. They are also harder to sand.

Two-Part Epoxy-Based Putties

Epoxy-based putties have the advantage of holding their shape, so that they can be sculpted without flowing. A water-soluble variety named Apoxie® Sculpt adheres to acrylic, polystyrene, wood, polyurethane and metal surfaces. It can be softened in warm water before use. Knead the two parts together and place in a warm cup of water for a few minutes. These putties can be sanded and worked with other tools after 12–24 hours, but the long drying period requires some extra planning and time. Wear rubber gloves when handling uncured two-part materials. Also use adequate ventilation when mixing.

This type of filler has the benefit of also being able to be used as a sculptural medium since it holds its own shape.

Staircasing on rapid prototyping parts (see Chapter 8, page 159) can be filled with polyfilla and sanded smooth to prepare for painting (above left). A small fan will speed up the drying (above centre), before sanding smooth with 220-grit sandpaper (above).

Pre-mixed water-based wood filler

Apoxie® Sculpt water-based epoxy two-part putty is structural and adheres to many substrates.

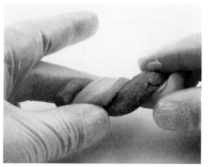

Part A and Part B are kneaded together by braiding and folding until colour is consistent.

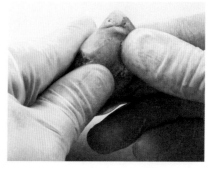

Wear rubber gloves to protect skin and help in clean-up.

Tutorial

Additive Modelling with Adhesives and Fillers

This tutorial of an abstract part shows how additive modelling is made possible by adhesives and fillers. A flat bottom piece will be joined to a top piece with a curved outline. Both parts are made out of polyurethane modelling board. The fillers will be used to shape an inside radius fillet that blends the two parts together at the joint line. Only water-soluble fillers have been used in this tutorial, including Apoxie® Sculpt for structure, followed by a polyfilla for the finish. The approach would be the same with automotive solvent-based body fillers, but would be faster. The first point is that the entire tutorial should be performed in a well-ventilated area such as under a fume hood, whether water-based or solvent-based materials are used.

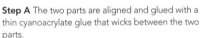

Step A The two parts are aligned and glued with a thin cyanoacrylate glue that wicks between the two parts.

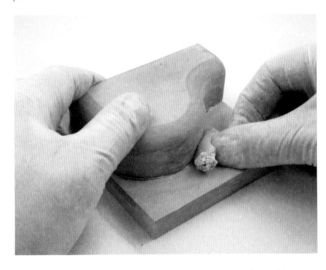

Step B Apoxie® Sculpt filler is mixed (see page 83) wearing disposable gloves, and then worked into the transition and smoothed with a custom-made styrene radius gauge (see Chapter 12, page 107).

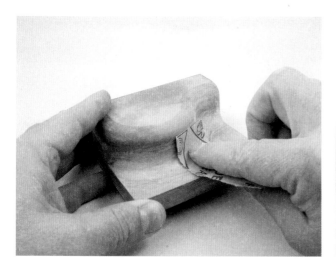

Step C The Apoxie® Sculpt is left to harden overnight and then sanded smooth.

Step D Quick-drying polyfilla is used for final finishing. The DryDex® brand of polyfilla contains a colourant so that it starts pink and hardens to a white colour.

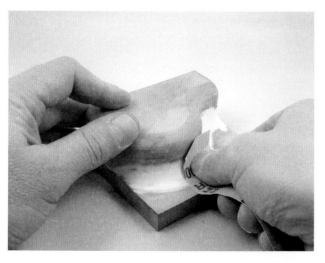

Step E Sanding with 400- and 600-grit sandpaper ensures complete smoothness. The final inside fillet radius is checked with a template. Filler application is repeated if necessary.

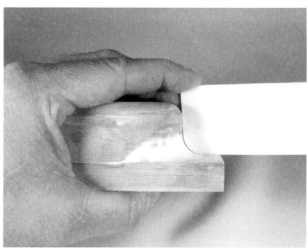

Step F The final shape should feel smooth and is then ready for priming. Half the model has been painted to show what the form will look like. A few coats of primer confirms whether more filling is necessary.

PAPER

Safety Check

— Read Chapter 5 on health and safety
— Use sharp blades and dispose of in a sharps container
— Use a steel rule as a guide and cut on a cutting mat

Paper comes in many forms and is categorized as sheet, cardboard or corrugated cardboard. It is a renewable, environmentally friendly, easy-to-work-with material. Since paper requires few tools it is both accessible and mobile. Its low-tech nature might create the perception that it is suitable mainly for craft projects, but it is actually an extremely flexible set of materials, more limited by skill and imagination than by its properties.

Julian Valle's impressive paper compositions show the exciting possibilities of using paper to create 3D designs.

Paper sheet comes in many different thicknesses and levels of shine and texture. Card stock is the thickest paper that can be cut with scissors and fed easily through a computer printer. Paper thicker than 0.5mm (0.02in) is classified as cardboard and is more easily cut with a scalpel on a cutting board than with scissors. Your local art shop will stock special high-quality cardboard for modelmaking such as mat board. For even more structural paper there is corrugated cardboard, available from companies that sell packaging materials, as well as from recycled scraps. It makes sense to reuse old materials when prototyping for exploration.

Applications for Paper

It is usually easy to draw conclusions about form and function in another material based on observing how a simple paper model behaves. For example, paper behaves in much the same way as sheet metal, but is much easier to use in a prototyping application. Paper studies of proportion and size, or the kinematic movement of mechanisms, as well as important packaging principles and collapsibility, are therefore common.

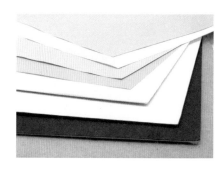

Paper comes in a variety of colours and thicknesses and can be worked without complicated tools.

Cantilevered Plywood Chair by Nicholas Kleemola, Carleton University, Ottawa (above). The small cardstock models in the background explored design solutions, whereas a full-scale cardboard prototype verified proportions and scale (left).

Paper prototypes often precede fabric prototypes when exploring new sewn products and are used in pattern creation.

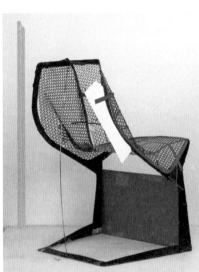

Konstantin Grcic uses paper and cardboard models as a tool to complement CAD and sketching.

A paper prototype is employed for user testing in the development of an interactive kiosk. Vector-based software (Illustrator®) and an inkjet printer allow detailed and realistic interfaces to be quickly prototyped.

Paper is also often the starting point for examining textiles, since it behaves in much the same way and allows us to create patterns. Chapter 20's discussion of soft goods products covers this in detail (see page 170).

Munich-based product designer Konstantin Grcic uses paper extensively to envision and sketch his ideas in three-dimensional space. He speaks passionately about how important it is to explore ideas in 1:1 scale in terms of both proportion and structure. Most studios do not have the facilities for making intricate and detailed models in final materials. This approach therefore makes use of a simple material to save time and to work any issues out as far as possible.

Digital 2D printing is a starting point of most prototyping, as will be shown in the next chapter on foamboard (pages 95–103). Even when the prototype is to be built in other materials it will often start with a printed template in paper. The computer is used to create layouts that are both accurately and instantly printed in colour. In interaction design, paper prototyping is used primarily to perform usability testing prior to developing computer code for interactive displays, so that the designers can try to predict the behaviour of the user.

Cross-Sectional Models

To create a surface representation of more complex geometry it is usually easier and more effective to make models from a series of cross sections. Such models approximate the shape as a series of slices and give a good idea of size and proportion.

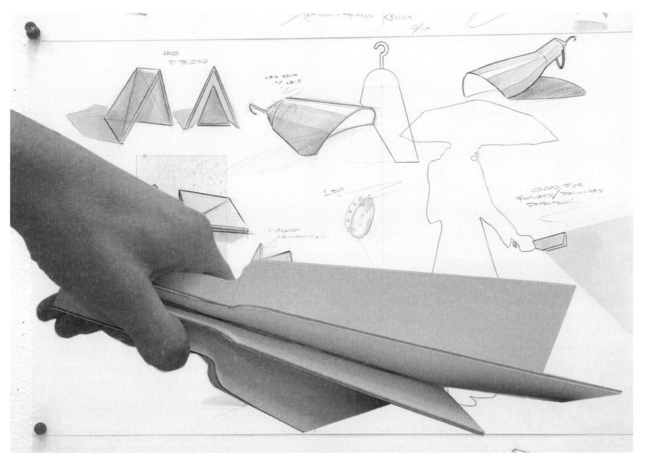

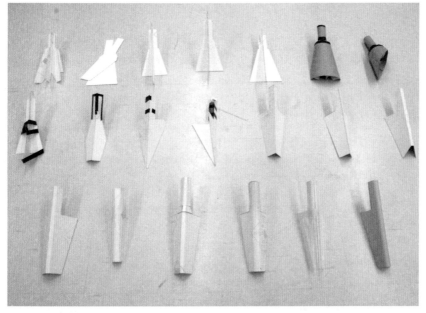

A cross-sectional model of a hand-held light accompanies concept sketches in order to gain a feel for the size and proportions (above). Quick paper models allows numerous formal iterations to be evaluated (left).

A dome can be approximated by a series of curved elements and overlapping glue tabs.

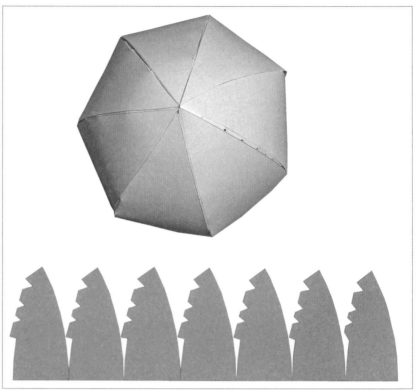

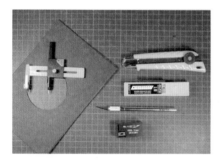

Stanley knives and scalpels are essential paper-modelling tools and should be kept sharp with an ample supply of replacement blades. Use a metal ruler and keep fingers away from the path of the cut.

Working with Paper and Board

In terms of creating three-dimensional forms the qualities of paper need to be understood. Paper can be cut, folded or twisted. It can be curved in one direction, which is suitable for geometric forms, such as cylinders and blocks. On the other hand, curvature in two directions would require the material to stretch. It is therefore not easy to create more complex forms such as spheres or organic forms in paper. A spherical shape can be approximated by a series of curved planes, as shown above.

Paper sheet can be cut with scissors or with a scalpel on a cutting mat. The self-healing cutting mat both guides the blade better and provides protection for underlying surfaces. Thick cardboard and corrugated cardboard are often cut with a Stanley knife. Always use extreme caution when handling these sharp instruments. A sharp blade is better than a dull blade as it will do the job with less force. Cardboard is never cut with one pass: usually three passes are necessary so as to cut the material accurately, cleanly and safely. Extra blades should be kept, and come in special containers that are also designed for safer sharps disposal. For straight cuts always use a metal ruler as a guide and make sure that fingers are not in the path of the cut.

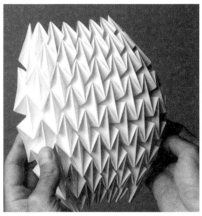

Paper folds from Paul Jackson's book *Folding Techniques for Designers*.

Paper folds can be used to explore the behaviour of sheet materials. More eloquent folding that builds on the techniques of origami can be used to explore three-dimensional form and collapsibility. Design educator Paul Jackson demonstrates these folding techniques in his book *Folding Techniques for Designers*.

Simple folds can be used for hinges and flaps. Board materials can also be folded with a metal ruler, and will bend more easily if the material has first been scored. Large curved surfaces are easily created by folding at regular intervals. Corrugated cardboard has flutes running in one direction and it is easier to create folds along these flutes.

When you need to join sheets together, tape is a quick option. It can also be used to hold sheets together while glue is drying. Rubber cement is an old-fashioned alternative to glue sticks but contains solvents and requires good ventilation, especially in a classroom setting when many people are using it at the same time. White-glue or hot-glue sticks create more structural joints with paperboard. White glue tends to result in cleaner work, but takes more time to dry. Tape or pins can be used to hold the work together while the white glue sets. Please refer to the Adhesives and Filler chapter for more detailed information (see page 79).

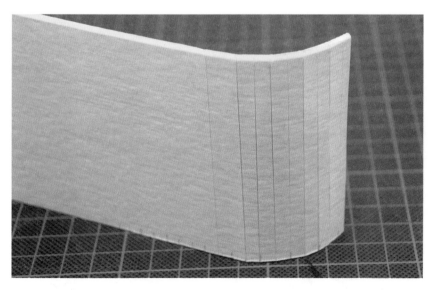

Curved surfaces are created by scoring and folding a series of bends.

Tutorial   Brent Toaster

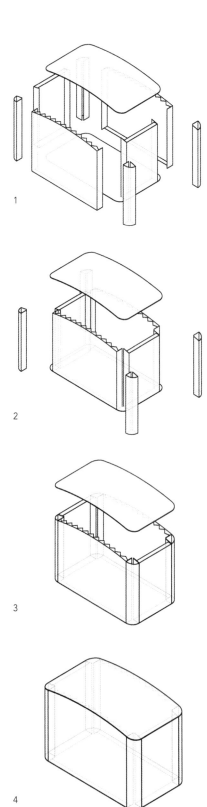

1

2

3

4

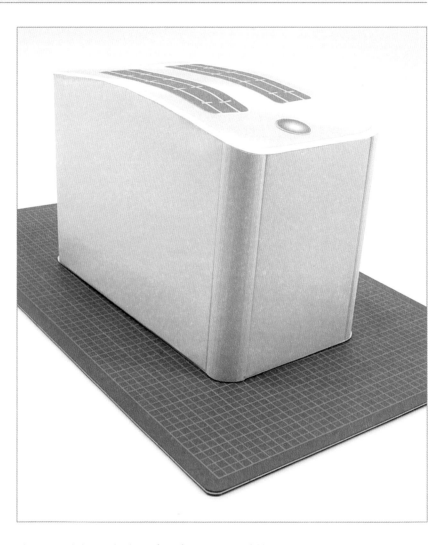

This tutorial shows the benefits of using an inkjet printer to create a visual model in paper. Even a quick model made in paper will be helpful for quickly evaluating overall shape and size. At the same time it is important to realize the limitations of paper; clever methods of folding can be used to create almost any geometry, but the return on invested time quickly diminishes. This example is probably at the limit of what it makes sense to do in paper. For more complex geometry it would be easier to create a cross-sectional model.

These drawings (numbered 1 to 4) show the sequence of construction. All pieces can be made directly from computer printouts, except the corner pieces, which are fabricated by curving pieces of paper. Note how tabs have been entered on the side panels to create stiffness and overlapping joints. Tabs along curved edges have to be notched in order to be folded.

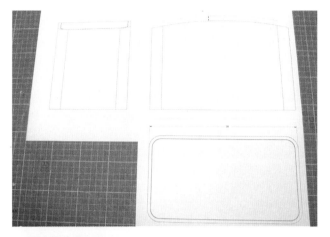

Step 1 Orthographic views of the toaster are created in either CAD or a vector-based program such as Illustrator®. These are printed on sheets of paper.

Step 2 In order to add some stiffness to the model, the bottom is glued to a piece of cardboard.

Step 3 Tabs are added manually by offsetting the edges by approximately 1cm (0.4in). Remember that the four vertical corners are shown on the side elevations, but are separate pieces. Tabs that run along curved sections are notched in order to allow them to be bent.

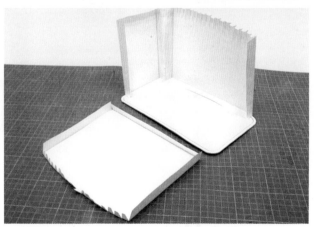

Step 4 The paper panels can now start to be assembled with glue. Tape is also used on the inside to hold the pieces together while they are drying.

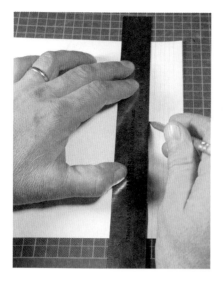
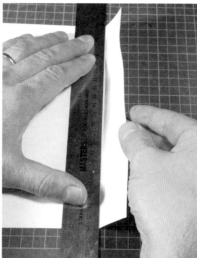
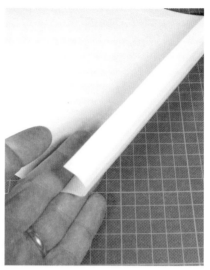

Step 5 The corner pieces are curved and cannot be created directly from the elevations. Instead, they are folded with a series of bends using a ruler to curve the paper.

Step 6 The resulting corner posts have to be trimmed to fit and are glued in place with tabs. Small clips or low-stick tape is used to hold the tabs together while drying. The corner posts could also easily have been made in polystyrene foam (see Chapter 14).

Step 7 You can create a high level of realism with a rendering done in Photoshop® and Illustrator®, using the simple techniques shown in the graphics chapter (see page 161). This view can be printed on glossy paper to capture some of the details and then trimmed and glued on to the top of the toaster.

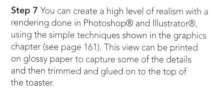

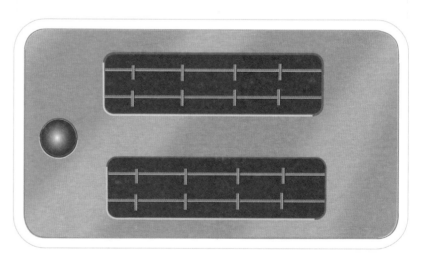

Foamboard

Safety Check

— Read Chapter 5 on health and safety
— Use sharp blades and dispose of in a sharps container
— Use a steel rule as a guide and cut on a cutting mat

Foamboard is a sheet material consisting of a Styrofoam core laminated between two layers of smooth paper, producing a lightweight yet rigid structure. It is available in various thicknesses typically ranging from 3mm to 13mm (1/8in to 1/2in), with 6mm (3/16in) being the most common choice. It is easier to work with and produces neater and stronger models than corrugated cardboard. This is because the foam centre produces a uniform solid edge that is also easy to cut. The best source for foamboard is the local art shop, which usually carries a range of thicknesses and sizes, but craft and stationery shops also tend to carry a small selection. Different colours are available, but the standard white is mostly used in practice because of its neutral colour.

Most geometric shapes can easily be created in foamboard. More advanced organic shapes can also be approximated by a series of cross sections as shown in the previous chapter (see page 89).

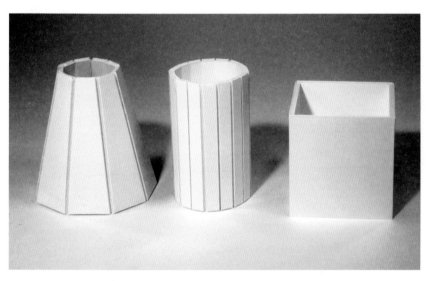

Foamboard is available in various colours and thicknesses.

Foamboard is used to study both form and function. The product's internal configuration is often prototyped by using real parts such as batteries, motors and other electronics in conjunction with foamboard. This gives the design team a good idea of assembly and fit. The Sonos ZonePlayer 120 is a wireless digital amplifier whose casing was developed by Y Studios in San Francisco. The designers made extensive use of foamboard in the design process, which allowed them to explore functional as well as visual aspects through this low-fidelity material. The assembly sequence was, for example, explored to test the viability of the product design intent. Real speaker connectors were added to study how they interfaced with the back panel and the circuit boards within. Thinner cardboard was used to simulate circuit boards, with polystyrene foam blocks standing in for electronic components. This example shows how low-fidelity materials can be modified rapidly, thus keeping the design process fluid. The designer gets a good feel of the proportions and complexity early in the process before the design progresses into 3D CAD development.

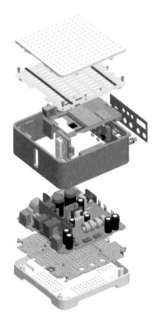

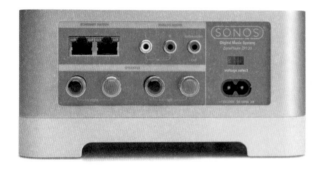

The Sonos ZonePlayer 120 wireless music streaming system was developed by Y Studios for Sonos Inc. in a process that included foamboard low-fidelity prototypes. The foamboard was combined with cardboard (for thinner components) and real off-the-shelf parts to examine assembly options.

Working with Foamboard

Foamboard is similar in function to corrugated cardboard, but more aesthetically pleasing. With a little bit of planning and skill, the foam edge can be hidden, producing neat, clean models. Cutting should always be done on a cutting mat and with a sharp scalpel or Stanley knife. It is a good idea to keep a box of extra blades handy, as these should be replaced at the slightest hint of wear. Most projects will require multiple blade replacements. Thicker-blade utility knives should be avoided, as they tend to crush the board and ruin the edge. The foamboard should always be cut with a minimum of three passes. The first goes through the top paper layer, the second cuts through the foam, and the last cuts through the bottom paper layer. Straight cuts are done with a metal ruler, whereas curves are cut carefully by hand.

Clean, sharp corners can easily be made to hide the core material and create a continuous exterior surface. Sharp corners at various angles can be made, as well as curved corners of various radii. The level of control over edges is much higher than with corrugated cardboard and is often a reason in itself for choosing this material. Hot glue is mostly used to glue parts together.

Cutting foamboard with a scalpel requires a steel ruler and several passes.

Corners

There are four types of corners: simple butt, bevel, folded and rabbet. These corner joints all have their own particular benefits.

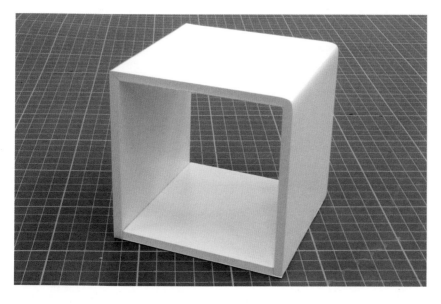

Cube with four types of corners: folded sharp (upper left), folded round (upper right), butt (lower left) and rabbet (lower right).

Butt Joint Corner

The simple butt joint is the fastest and most efficient corner, though it exposes the foam from one board. For exploratory work or functional test prototypes this type of joint is often satisfactory.

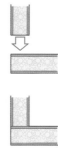

Folded Round Corner

The foamboard is scored on the inside with a partial cut and then bent. This compresses and crushes the core while stretching the outside paper layer enough to create a rounded edge roughly equal to the board thickness.

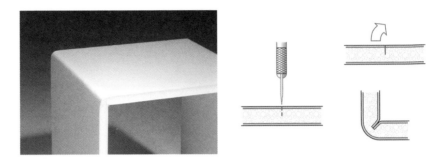

Folded Sharp Corner

By cutting out a wedge-shaped V-notch of foam, the board can be bent into a tight corner. Obtuse and acute angles are also possible and can be graphically calculated by drawing a V-shaped groove to the required angle on the end of the board. The wedge is then carefully cut so that the blade does not cut through the bottom layer of paper. Bevelled or mitred corners can also be made by mating two different parts that have been trimmed at an angle. In this case each piece would be trimmed to half the total angle.

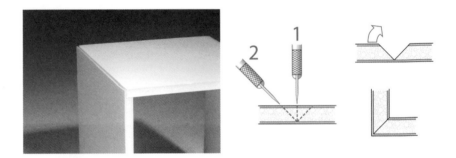

Rabbet Corner

The rabbet corner involves removing a slot in one of the parts, which the other part fits into, effectively hiding the joint. It is especially useful in situations where a piece of foamboard is made to fit over a curve (see tutorial).

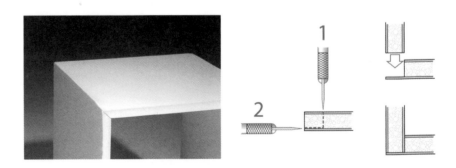

Curves

Curved planes and cylinders are formed by approximation. A series of tight folds creates a curve as a series of straight segments. The simplest approach is to score the material at regular intervals and then bend it so that the cuts are on the outside. If a smooth exterior surface is desired then the folds should be on the inside. This usually requires a series of V-notches so that the material can be folded more easily.

Cylinders and curves are formed by a series of folds. These can be external or internal (above, left and right). The fold spacing affects the smoothness, as shown above.

Tutorial

Train Ticket Kiosk

The large size of a product such as a ticket kiosk makes foamboard a convenient and inexpensive modelling material. This tutorial will highlight techniques that hide the edges of the foam and use custom-rendered decals to illustrate details such as screens and buttons. For the purposes of the tutorial, the model will be built at quarter scale. A full-scale model would be built in the same way using the same materials.

Step 1 A full-scale 2D rendering is created in Illustrator®. The rendering uses a side profile of a person to help govern the placement of the screen.

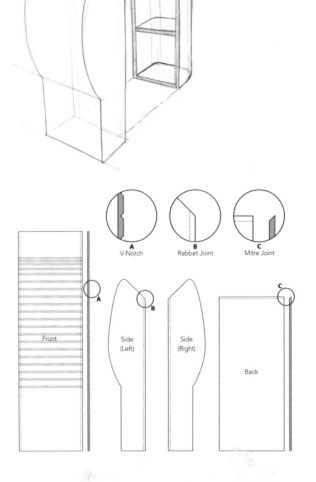

Step 2 This exploded sketch shows that the kiosk model consists of two sections: a curved front interactive panel and a rear housing section. In terms of manufacturing we are simulating a product that would be made out of plastic and sheet metal.

Step 3 Template patterns are created in Illustrator® using the rendered illustration as an underlay. Five separate pieces are needed for the display section. Dashed lines are used to indicate cuts that do not go through the entire board.

A
V-Notch

B
Rabbet Joint

C
Mitre Joint

Front

Side (Left)

Side (Right)

Back

Step 4 Each pattern is printed on regular bond paper to one-quarter scale. These are then glued directly on to the foamboard. A sharp scalpel is used to cut out each piece of the model with a three-stroke approach.

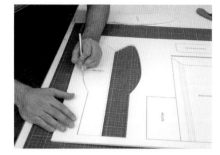 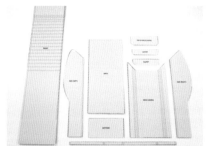

Front Panel Step 1 Trim rabbet joints on side pieces using a metal ruler. These channels will hide the edge of the back foamboard piece.

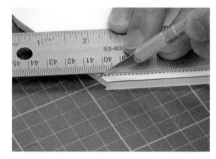 

Front Panel Step 2 Rabbet cuts are made on each side of the front piece to accept the two side pieces and hide the edge of the foam. The front piece is then scored with V-notches on the inside at 1cm (0.4in) intervals to allow the surface to curve.

Front Panel Step 3 Attach the side pieces to the rear piece with hot glue. Apply the glue to the rabbet cut and hold while glue dries. Attaching the sides to the back first will make it easier to attach the curved front piece.

Front Panel Step 4 The front piece is now glued on by working from the back. In this case the glue is added carefully to the untrimmed edge, as it is easier to control. Glue small sections at a time, being careful with the amount of glue, so it does not seep out the edge. Note how extra scoring lines were added to the section that wraps around the tight corner.

Rear Housing Step 1 The sides and back are created in one piece of foamboard. The rear corners are rounded, which requires three V-notches to be removed on both corners.

Rear Housing Step 2 Rounded gussets are glued in to help define the rounded corners and add strength.

 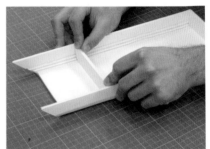

Rear Housing Step 3 The curved top is glued on after the rabbet joint has been prepared all around the piece.

Final Assembly Step 1 The back is secured in place with hot glue.

Final Assembly Step 2 The final step is to glue on the decal that captures the interactive elements of the self-serve kiosk. Spray glue works well, but should be used only in a spray booth or outdoors. Double-sided tape or rubber cement are suitable substitutes.

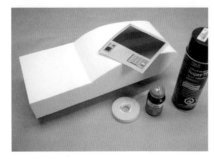 

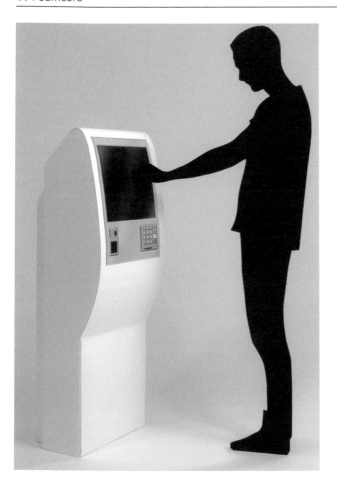

The final model is shown with a scale person interacting with the machine. The scale person was cut out from the initial Illustrator® outline on black foamboard. The composition below was created by superimposing the photo on to a background scene in Photoshop®.

POLYSTYRENE FOAM

12

Safety Check

— Read Chapter 5 on health and safety
— If hotwire is used, use only in well-ventilated areas and exhaust all fumes. Do not touch hotwire as it will burn fingers
— Obtain professional training and supervision before using power or machine tools
— Wear a dust mask and use a dust-collection system, or vacuum frequently when sanding
— Read SDS information

Closed-cell polystyrene foam is an inexpensive and easily worked material for low-fidelity form exploration work. It is made by infusing polystyrene plastic with gas during the manufacturing process. Although its main use is in housing insulation or product packaging, it is also very popular as a desktop modelmaking material since it can be sculpted quickly with the simplest of tools. This material is suitable for complex forms made by a subtractive sculptural process. The iterative mindset reigns when working in polystyrene foam. A fluid process allows the designer to move between hand sketching, foam modelling and digital modelling so as to keep the ideas flowing.

Complex forms are quickly explored and sculpted in polystyrene foam.

XPS foam sheets are sold in various thicknesses and colours.

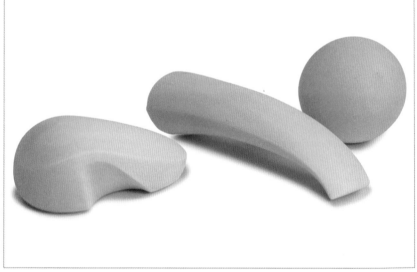

Expanded polystyrene foam is less suitable as a modelling material owing to its beaded construction.

There are two different kinds of polystyrene foam. Extruded foam (XPS) – or Styrofoam – is a readily available solid insulation material sold in various thickness sheets by builder's merchants. Depending on the supplier, it will be manufactured in different colours, including pink, blue or white. It may also be purchased as thicker pallets from specialty suppliers. The low density of the material 40kg/m3 (2lb/ft3) makes it extremely easy to work with.

Expanded polystyrene foam (EPS) is the second kind, and is essentially the same material except it consists of beads that are pre-expanded and then fused together with steam. This manufacturing process is suitable for making moulded shapes and is frequently used in product packaging. EPS is typically white in colour. The beaded construction also makes it harder to work with than XPS, as the beads tend to break off and create unsmooth edges and surfaces. It is therefore inferior to XPS as a modelling material.

Applications for Polystyrene Foam

Polystyrene foam is suitable where speed and a lower level of fidelity are needed. Exploration of form and overall visual proportion is a typical application. Although not very strong it is sometimes used in early user testing of ergonomics and fit. The main benefit is the low cost and the fact that it can be worked with simple hand tools into complex forms right at the designer's desktop. The speed with which foam can be worked also allows multiple variations to be realized and evaluated side by side.

For larger models it is often more cost-effective and easy to handle than other, heavier modelling materials. Polystyrene foam is, for example, used to verify tool paths for CNC machining as the material is inexpensive and can be cut quickly before investing in a more expensive machining board.

Foam is a fast and effective material for early form explorations, as shown in this extensive model by Nancy Mistove for Funrise Toys. Surface details and visual interest are added with marker pen and simple paper labels.

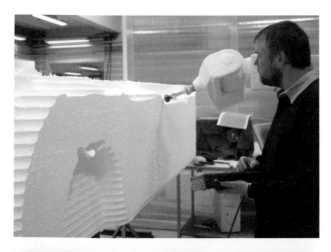

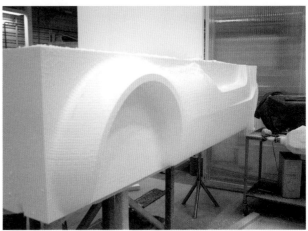

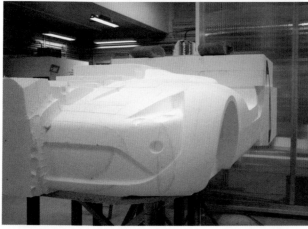

Polystyrene foam does, however, have limitations. The low density and soft structure means that it is easily dented and will not hold fine details. For ergonomic testing the material does not exhibit the final product weight properly and if weighted it will be prone to breaking. Polystyrene foam models are generally unpainted, or painted only in a neutral colour such as white. This is usually appropriate for low-fidelity prototypes and avoids unnecessary discussion about product details at the early stage of a project.

A full-size foam model of the Olme Spyder sports car is CNC machined in polystyrene foam at Umeå Institute of Design, Sweden.

Working with Polystyrene Foam

Shaping

Polystyrene is a thermoplastic. This means that under heat the material will become flexible and then melt. It can therefore be easily shaped and cut with a low-voltage electric tool known as a hotwire. Several advancements have been made to hotwire technology, including hand-held tools that add flexibility and carving potential for a finer level of detail. These specialty tools are worth the investment if you want to make a great many foam models. Hotwire tools do, however, cause the plastic to melt and emit toxic fumes. Good ventilation is therefore necessary.

Hotwire tools cut through polystyrene foam as if it were butter. The fume hood shown in the picture is essential in order to remove the fumes given off as the styrene melts.

In addition to hotwire tools, rasps and sandpaper are used to shape accurate surfaces. In the example below, a polystyrene foam sphere is shaped with successively finer tools. Start by cutting a cylinder that has the same diameter as the sphere (see picture above). The height should also be equal to the sphere diameter. If necessary, laminate two or more sections of polystyrene foam together to attain the necessary thickness. The rasp is used for the initial rough removal of material followed by a coarse-grit sandpaper to establish overall form. The final smoothing is done with medium-grit sandpaper. The sphere is made perfectly round by using a sanding template of the correct radius. The sanding template is made from foam as well with a fine-grit sandpaper glued to the inside radius.

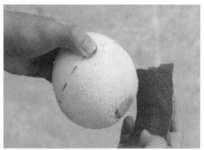

A polystyrene sphere is made by rasping the overall shape, followed by successively finer grades of sandpaper and a sanding template.

Masking tape can be used as a sanding mask to control transitions. The foam sands more easily than the tape and thus helps create an edge. Simple templates are used to check radii and curvatures.

Taping and sanding an edge radius. The radius is checked with a radius gauge.

The computer should be used where it saves time and makes the work easier and more productive. This can be as basic as creating outlines in Illustrator® and then printing them out on paper, which is then affixed as a cutting outline.

Remember to think additively. It is easier to make bits and pieces and add them together, rather than try to carve everything out of a solid block. Sometimes the designer may wish to add a little more material to thicken a surface or change a detail. Plasticine can be used in cases of quick exploration as it can be easily added on top of foam, although it cannot be painted. Sometimes a section of the model will be cut away and replaced with a new piece. This deconstructive approach is very common in explorative work and creates a fluid workflow that is open to changing and examining variations on the design.

Gluing

White paper glue or carpenter's glue (which is very similar) and rubber cement are used for laminating sheets together for thicker models as well as to affix labels or decals. Thin amounts of spray glue will also work, but this is a less environmentally-friendly option. For attaching small pieces or detail, cyanoacrylate glues will work well.

Solvent-based glues such as contact cement should not be used as they will chemically eat through the polystyrene foam and ruin the work. Hot glue melts the foam surface upon contact. Hardened hot glue also presents problems for cutting and sanding, as it is harder than the foam.

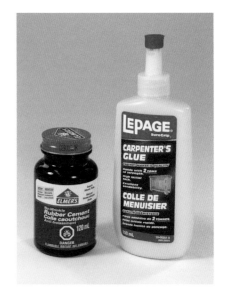

Carpenter's glue or paper glues such as rubber cement and white glue work best for polystyrene foam.

Water-based polyfillas are suitable as they do not react chemically with the polystyrene foam and they sand as easily as the foam itself.

Fillers and Paint

It is generally preferable to avoid filling and painting polystyrene foam. A simple unpainted model made quickly for a formal study should not be painted just to make it look more realistic. In fact this extra step not only creates extra work, but also may detract from the exploratory nature and advantages of the material. Water-based polyfilla-type fillers work best as they do not melt the foam and they will sand about as easily as the foam itself. They are suitable only for filling small areas, such as when creating an inside radius.

When polystyrene foam prototypes are finished and painted it is usually only to hide fillers with a coat of primer or for preliminary colour studies. Paints should be water-based and preferably flat. This is because a flat finish will not show surface defects or paint strokes as easily. Even if the final product is intended to be glossy, it is usually understood that these models are exploratory. The primer coat is usually water-based gesso, a particle-filled paint used to seal canvas for subsequent painting. This is usually applied with a good brush. When it dries it may be sanded with fine sandpaper and then painted with a water-based acrylic paint, applied by hand, roller or airbrush. Water-based acrylic primers will also work.

Spray bombs and oil-based paints will eat through the surface of the model. Many students learn the hard way and end up having to rebuild the model from scratch.

Gesso or primer is applied with a foam brush.

Detailing

Foam is a low-fidelity material. Finer product details such as parting lines, buttons and screens are not made effectively in polystyrene foam. These are instead usually added in the form of two-dimensional labels that both save time and look better on these low-fidelity prototypes. Graphic design tape can be used effectively to visualize parting lines.

For early study models, markers may be used directly on the surface of the model (see image of toy study on page 105). For a more refined appearance, a label is designed in Adobe Illustrator® or Painter™. These are printed on paper and then glued on to the foam model. Often regular bond paper is preferred to glossy stock as it is thinner and easier to apply. The Walkie-Talkie tutorial below illustrates these benefits clearly. Refer to Chapter 19 on graphics (see page 161) to see the label-making process in detail.

Tutorial

Children's Walkie-Talkie

This tutorial will show you how to make a model in XPS foam. Small details such as the LCD and buttons will be illustrated on paper labels designed in Illustrator® and printed on a regular inkjet printer. The labels and lack of paint both save time and keep the workmanship clean and crisp.

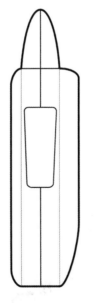

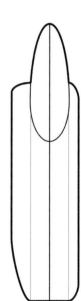

Overview The model consists of a main body and an antenna. The main body has a top surface that is blended between the flat-top LCD plane and a horizontal plane A that demarcates the flat side contour. The antenna has an elliptical cross section.

Step 1 A full-scale 2D rendering layout is created in Illustrator® (see page 163). Alternatively, this could be hand-drawn (for a very quick model) or created in CAD. This drawing will be used as a template for foam cutting and sanding. The labels for the LCD display and speaker grill will also be printed from this file.

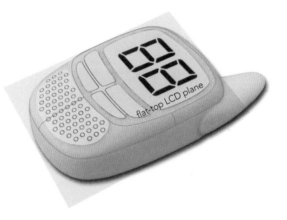

Main Body Step 1 The top view of the model is glued to the foam with glue stick or rubber cement (these types of glue allow the label to be peeled off later). Next the profile is cut using a hotwire, leaving a little extra material for finishing. Be sure to do some testing with feed and voltage on a scrap piece beforehand. The outline could also be cut on a bandsaw, scroll saw or even by hand.

Main Body Step 2 The hotwire trims the part to size, but leaves a coarse outline. The extra millimetre of material should be left so that it can be smoothed with 320-grit sandpaper. The top outline template will be peeled off for the next step.

 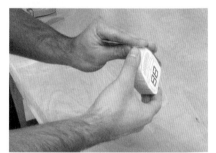

Main Body Step 3 In order to create the convex top surface, the transition is marked with masking tape. A top label is also added that defines the top LCD plane.

Main Body Step 4 The convex top surface is carefully shaped with 320-grit sandpaper. Since the paper label resists sanding more than the foam, the transitions are kept crisp and clean.

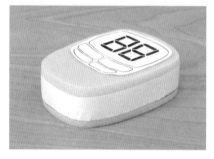 

Main Body Step 5 A side-profile template can be used to check that the profile is as intended. This step is not strictly needed, but helps maintain a predefined shape. A new top label will later need to be printed and applied, since the label has been sacrificed during sanding.

Antenna Step 1 The top and side views of the antenna are cut out and affixed to a piece of foam.

Antenna Step 2 Both profiles are now cut on the hotwire. The elliptical cross section is sanded by hand.

 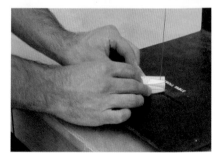

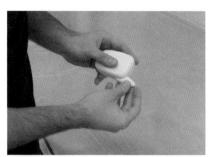

Antenna Step 3 The final elliptical antenna is checked against the main body for fit.

Final Assembly Step 1 New labels are printed and trimmed. The model is now ready for final assembly with rubber cement. White paper glue will also work well.

Final Assembly Step 2 Printed labels are affixed.

Final Assembly Step 3 Thin graphic design tape is applied to define the parting line as shown.

THERMOPLASTIC SHEET AND EXTRUDED SHAPES

Safety Check

— Read Chapter 5 on health and safety
— Obtain professional training and supervision before using power or machine tools
— Wear a dust mask and use a dust-collection system, or vacuum frequently when sanding
— Read SDS information

Thermoplastics include common household materials such as ABS, acrylic, polystyrene, polypropylene and polycarbonate. These plastics become liquid when heated to their viscous melting temperature, allowing for mass-production injection-moulding. Thermoplastics are also extruded or cast into different sizes of tubing and sheet, readily available through commercial retailers for fabrication.

Polystyrene and acrylic sheet and tubing are available in a range of sizes, colours and finishes.

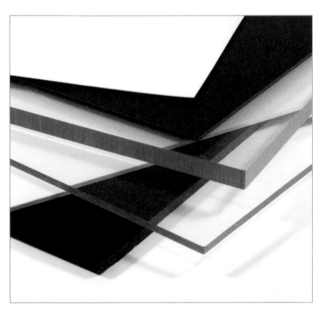

Acrylic (Perspex®) and polystyrene are especially easy to work with and make versatile, general-use modelmaking materials. Other plastics are used mostly for their particular properties: for example, polycarbonate (Lexan™) is tough and impact-resistant, whereas polypropylene is chemically resistant (which also makes it hard to glue or paint).

Plastic is an appropriate material for additive modelling, since pieces of tubing and sheet can be cut and combined with other materials, as well as with custom-printed parts.

Being creative with sourcing materials can save a great deal of time and money on a project. ABS drainpipe, available from building material retailers, is, for example a suitable and inexpensive modelling material. Polystyrene sheet and extrusions made by Evergreen Scale Models are available in hobby shops internationally. These shapes also have the benefit of being designed to telescope.

Plastic is a very versatile material and is therefore used for both low- and high-fidelity models. In my own experience I have often used plastic for proof of works-like prototypes that augment my thinking when sketching and using 3D CAD. Polystyrene (often simply referred to as styrene) is particularly easy to work with and to create working prototypes of mechanisms. It is easy to add and subtract material in an ongoing fashion so as to test the mechanism. Two-dimensional CAD drawings can be transferred to sheets of styrene and cut out with a scroll saw or bandsaw.

This approach is shown in a project for Dana Douglas, a company specializing in products for the home healthcare market, such as mobility aids. The challenge was to rethink the brake mechanisms on rollators (rolling walkers). On previous products, brake handles were connected to brake levers on the rear wheels via bicycle-type cables. The problem was that the cables could possibly snag on door handles and other obstructions. The objective was therefore to develop an internal rod-activated braking system without cables.

These student projects incorporate clear plastic elements as part of their design. These high-fidelity appearance models make use of clear acrylic sheet.

Evergreen Scale Models styrene extrusions and sheets are available in a range of sizes. They also are useful for telescoping structures (above).

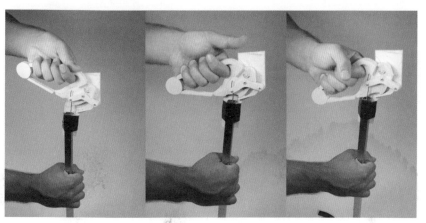

A proof-of-concept model brake mechanism made from styrene sheet. This handmade works-like prototype could be altered quickly to better understand the design parameters for a new internal brake mechanism for a rollator (rolling walker).

The learning gained from the styrene model was translated into a SolidWorks® 3D CAD model and 3D prototypes were printed for design verification (far right). The final rollator with internal brake mechanism is shown at right.

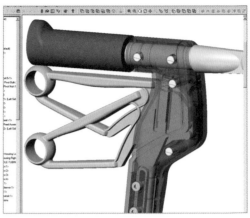

Explorative work with sketches and simple 2D CAD and paper models progressed toward a simple works-like prototype made out of styrene. This made it much easier to develop an understanding of feasibility. The 3D CAD development was not initiated until the design parameters were better understood, utilizing the simple styrene prototype.

Working with Plastics

Plastic sheet and shapes are worked through both manual and digital means. Thinner sections of styrene can be worked right on the desktop with a scalpel, whereas thicker materials typically require some power tools. Technologies such as laser cutting allow intricate outlines to be realized from simple 2D Illustrator® drawing files.

Cutting

Thin styrene sheet and extrusions are very easily cut with hand tools. Sheet is usually scored and then broken. Curved outlines in sheet up to 1.5mm (1/16in) can be cut with a scalpel, by tracing an outline in several passes. Thicker materials need to be sawed.

Thin styrene sheet is easily scored and then snapped (left), or cut with a scalpel (right) for curved outlines.

Acrylic and polycarbonate sheets are usually supplied with a paper or plastic protective cover that can be used to lay out a cutting outline. Intricate outlines can be cut quickly and effectively from a 2D Illustrator® file with laser cutters. Lasers can also deboss patterns and images, allowing for even greater design creativity.

CNC machining is used to machine complex geometry parts in plastic. This is often necessary when creating parts where the exact material qualities are required. Rapid prototyping materials are approximate and may not be applicable in all situations.

Gluing Plastics

Plastics are unique in that they can be solvent-bonded. The solvent melts the plastic, allowing molecules to move from one part to be joined to the other. The limitation is that only similar materials can be joined. However, many of these solvents are toxic and it is critical to read the SDS information for the glue. Cyanoacrylate (super glue) is a popular modelmaking glue and will also allow dissimilar materials to be joined (see Chapter 14, page 125). Polypropylene and polyethylene are virtually impossible to glue and should instead be mechanically joined with screws or rivets.

Filling

The fillers used with plastics are identical to those suitable for polyurethane modelling boards. Plastic parts can therefore easily be blended with other materials and painted smooth.

Painting and Finishing

Styrene can be painted to simulate many other materials, including metals. It is often easier to make parts in styrene and paint them in a metal finish than to make parts in steel or aluminium. This can be a useful simulation for appearance models, as shown in the tutorial at the end of this chapter.

Thermoforming

Heated thermoplastics reach a soft, formable state at a temperature referred to as the glass transition point. ABS, acrylic and styrene reach this glass transition point at a much lower temperature than their viscous melting temperatures. Heat can therefore be easily used to form thermoplastic amorphous materials such as styrene into various shapes. The simplest form of thermoforming is with a heat gun or heat bender. The material is heated and then set in a form or simply clamped into shape until it cools and sets.

Acrylic can be cut quickly and accurately using a laser cutter.

Fine-detail CNC-machined ABS prototype. These parts were machined with a very fine-ball end-mill cutter (1.5mm/0.06in dia.).

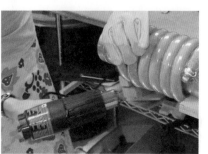

A barbecue utensil is heat-formed with a strip heater and hand-held heat gun. Plastic tubes can be thermoformed without collapsing by first filling them with sand and capping the ends (left).

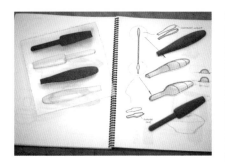

Vacuum forming is a simple and economical approach to making clear plastic parts or multiples using basic tools made from wood or polyurethane board.

Vacuum Forming

More complex three-dimensional shapes can be created with vacuum forming, using simple handmade or CNC-machined tooling. This is also a good method for creating multiple parts and a more economical way for students to prototype larger parts than is usually feasible through 3D printing. In industry, vacuum forming is used to produce anything from packaging to larger plastic panels such as refrigerator doors. The advantage of this method is that it is a low-pressure process that requires only simple moulds and equipment. The basic ingredients are: a sheet of plastic held in a rigid frame, a mould (to shape the plastic over), an oven and a vacuum source to pull the heated plastic sheet over the mould.

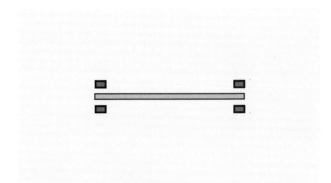

Stage 1: Sheet material is clamped in a metal frame.

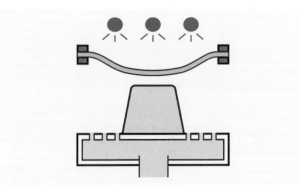

Stage 2: The sheet material is heated until it starts to sag and is then brought over the mould (shown in green).

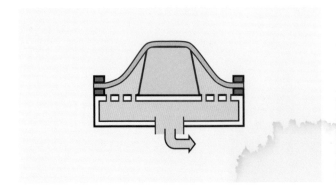

Stage 3: The material is stretched over the mould, making an airtight seal between the mould base and the clamping frame.

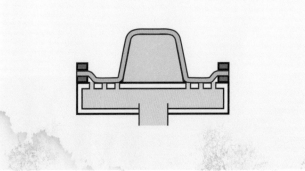

Stage 4: Vacuum is applied, sucking the plastic tight against the mould. The part is then removed and trimmed of excess plastic.

Positive male moulds are more commonly used, but since the material is pulled on top of the mould, the material offset makes all the edges and corners smooth. The thicker the material, the more pronounced the effect. Negative female moulds are created by machining a cavity, into which the heated plastic material is pulled. Negative moulds are usually more complex to manufacture, but offer the benefit of capturing sharp details on the exterior of the vacuum-formed part.

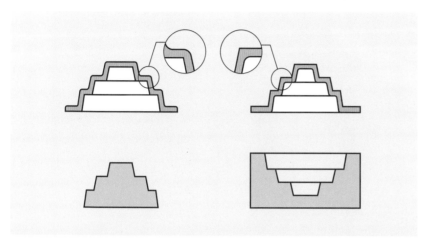

Parts produced on positive moulds have rounded edges (left), whereas negative moulds will allow sharp detail to be transferred to the outside of the part (right).

In order to be able to remove the plastic after forming, it is important to follow some specific rules for vacuum forming. Plastic materials will shrink when cooled, so the tools are usually built slightly oversized incorporating the shrinkage rate (this varies from plastic to plastic, but 1 per cent is not unusual). The walls of the tool should have a taper since the plastic shrinks onto the tool as it cools. The taper, also known as a draft angle, enables the part to be removed. Draft angles of 3 to 5 degrees are advisable. The tool must also not have any geometry that has a negative angle or overhang. This situation, also known as an undercut, will permanently lock the part onto the tool. Deeper parts may have problems such as webbing or thinning. Negative moulds require less draft (since material will shrink away from walls) and tend to prevent webbing from occurring. For larger and more extensive projects the references listed at the end of the book may prove useful.

Case Study Adaptive Ski System

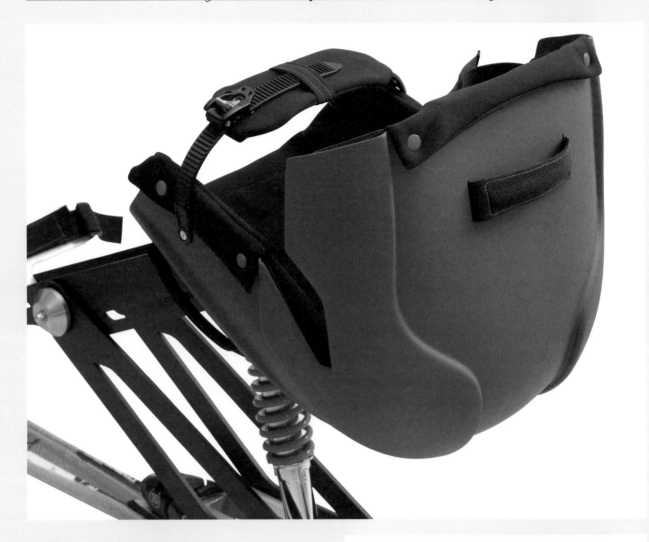

This final-year project by Mike Defazio (Carleton University, Ottawa), for an adaptive ski system was carried out in collaboration with the Canadian Paralympic Foundation. The ski included a specially designed seat that had to be prototyped in plastic. 3D printing would have been very expensive given the size of the part. Using a wooden mould made in the university shop and utilizing both traditional as well as CNC machining, the part could be vacuum formed at the school's vacuum-forming facilities. A series of experimental pulls was required to identify problems with webbing and other typical vacuum-forming issues. The final part was then trimmed and final details such as straps and fittings were added.

This adaptive ski system for disabled skiers incorporated a prototype seat made with vacuum-formed plastic (see pages 116 and 119).

The vacuum-forming mould was made by laminating pieces of wood and shaping with rasps, sanders and templates.

A clamped sheet of styrene plastic is heated under the vacuum-forming oven until it starts sagging and is then pulled down over the positive plug by the vacuum and cooled into shape.

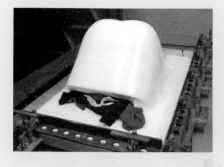

Large vacuum-forming projects require some experimentation in order to achieve proper pulls. With the bugs worked out, the black piece (middle) is ready to be trimmed and painted for the final model (right).

Tutorial   Barbecue Utensil

The following tutorial shows how plastic sheet and extrusions can be used to prototype various parts and simulate different materials. An appearance model of a barbecue spatula was made from acrylic sheet and an extruded plastic pipe. Metal was simulated with metallic paint and the rubber handle was simulated with flat paint (rubber appears flat). The focus here was to study and communicate appearance rather than functionality.

Planning: The initial design is planned with sketches and drawings as well as very quick full-scale explorative prototypes in cardboard to establish overall proportions as well as the proper ergonomic angle of the spatula.

Spatula Step 1 The spatula shape is cut out from acrylic sheet on a laser cutter. Two variations of the design are initially cut out to examine visual alternatives. The file for the laser cutter is an Illustrator® drawing.

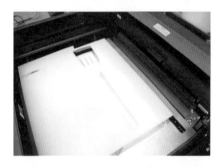

Spatula Step 2 A chamfer is added with a file and then sanded smooth. This would have been difficult to achieve in metal and would have required machine tools.

Spatula Step 3 The spatula is now bent using heat. First the plastic is heated on the exact line of the bend using a strip heater (far left). When the plastic softens it is carefully bent using a piece of wood as a forming jig (left).

Rubber Handles Step 1 The rubber handle pieces are simulated using a plastic tube. The cross sections of the handle pieces correspond to a section of a cylinder. 3.8cm (1.5in) diameter plastic tubing is trimmed on a bandsaw. It is essential to have adequate training and supervision when using power equipment such as a bandsaw. Note how the lateral push stick has a V-notch taken out of it to hold the circular tube better.

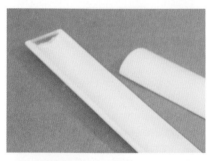

Rubber Handles Step 2 To make the handle pieces appear solid the ends are capped off with a semicircular section of plastic glued on with cyanoacrylate glue. These parts are now ready for primer and paint.

Paint Step 1 The parts are primed with acrylic water-based primer using an airbrush or small paint gun.

Paint Step 2 The spatula is painted with a metallic water-based paint to simulate metal. The handles are painted in a flat black colour to simulate rubber. Several thin coats are used to ensure good coverage without drips.

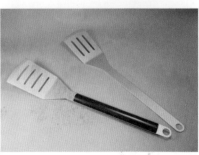

Final Assembly The handles could easily be glued to the spatula at this point. By using double-sided tape, however, it is possible to transfer the handles from one spatula to the next, so as to evaluate the two options side by side.

POLYURETHANE MODELLING BOARD

Safety Check

— Read Chapter 5 on health and safety
— Obtain professional training and supervision before using power or machine tools
— Wear a dust mask and use a dust-collection system or vacuum frequently when sanding
— Read SDS information

Polyurethane (PU) modelling board is a high-quality material that can be sculpted to a fine level of detail and finish. Specifically developed for applications to replace wood, it is dimensionally stable, does not have a grain structure and will not rot. The density is consistent and available in specific increments. In addition to its use in modelmaking it is used as a coring material in marine and aviation applications. Being a thermoset plastic material, it has strong polymer bonds and is generally not heat formable. Polyurethane boards are distinguished primarily by density. The lower-density materials, often referred to as foam, are easier to shape, but have visible surface porosity. This is not generally an issue for low-fidelity prototypes, where a porous surface texture conveys the correct message that the model is not final. Higher-density modelling boards, sometimes called machining boards, tend to have a density higher than 480kg/m3 (30lb/ft3).

Applications for Polyurethane Board

The lower-density materials are good for explorative work, whereas higher-density boards are excellent for highly refined appearance prototypes. The higher-density materials are also useful for making tools for vacuum forming (see page 116).

Product designers use polyurethane modelling board extensively for form development. The speed and efficacy at which the material can be hand-worked or CNC machined means that prototypes can be built quickly and that many different options can be studied in real physical space.

Take, for example, the iconic One Laptop Per Child (OLPC) project. Yves Béhar and his firm Fuseproject were given a demanding brief by Nicholas Negroponte, who initiated the OLPC project at MIT's Media Lab. This low-cost laptop specifically aimed to make computing and Wi-Fi technology available to children in developing countries, demanding ruggedness, portability and the ability to recharge in locations that may have no electricity supply. Fuseproject started by focusing on the experience of the product in terms of an overall product strategy. The product had to be intuitive and friendly-looking. During ensuing ideation, a fluid approach that used sketching, 3D CAD and prototyping concurrently allowed an examination of different options against the design objectives and strategy. In all, more than 40 different prototypes were built. Polyurethane modelling board was a useful and easy-to-use material for looking at a series of formal variations, as shown below.

Polyurethane board/foam in densities ranging from 80 to 320kg/m3 (6– 20lb/ft3) is shown on the left (yellow), while polyurethane machining board ranging from 480 to 800kg/m3 (30– 50lb/ft3) in density is shown on the right.

240kg/m3 (15lb/ft3) PU foam (left) and 480kg/m3 (30lb/ft3) machining board (right) are common low- and high-fidelity material choices respectively.

Fuseproject made more than 40 prototypes, many of them in PU, during the development of the One Laptop Per Child computer project. Sketches and computer work went hand in hand with prototypes to explore and test many alternatives.

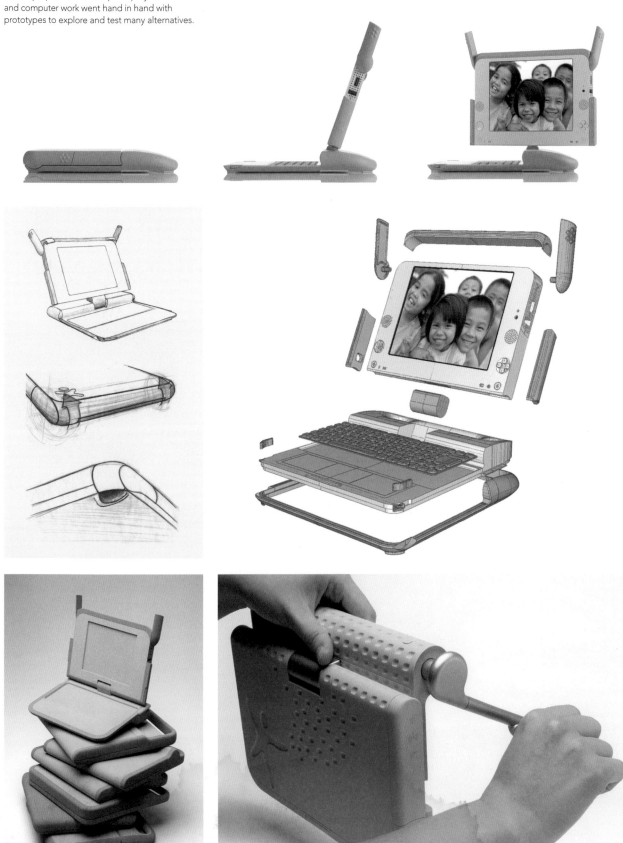

Working with PU Modelling Board

Polyurethane dust is very fine and will easily become airborne, so containment and personal protection against the dust is important. Always wear eye protection and a dust mask, and be careful not to rub your eyes accidentally with dusty hands. Avoid blowing air to clean up: instead rely on vacuuming and containment. The higher-density machining boards are generally formulated to produce less dust, as they have more binders than the low-density foams.

Hand-Shaping PU Modelling Board

Lower-density PU modelling board (foam) can be cut and shaped easily with hand tools. A three-step process is an effective way to work with different grades of polyurethane foam – this involves cutting, followed by shaping and then finishing. Cutting usually starts with cutting an outline with a bandsaw. Hotwire tools will not work since the material is not a thermoplastic and therefore will not melt. Hand saws, also, are able easily to cut lower-density materials. Shaping is done with a rasp to rough the shape. This saves time and creates far less dust than trying to sand the shape. Some extra material should be left on the part for finishing with sandpaper.

The three-step approach as shown here involves cutting with a saw, shaping with a rasp and finishing with sandpaper.

CNC Machining

Polyurethane foams are machined very accurately with a CNC machine. The higher-density machining boards have been specifically developed to be CNC machined and to produce less dust while cutting. Professional modelmaking shops specialize in producing highly realistic appearance prototypes for a range of clients in industry. These shops employ highly trained professional modelmakers who are specialized in creating precision prototypes, including all aspects of final detailing. Professional designers tend to focus on making initial prototypes in-house and subcontract the final high-quality appearance prototypes to a modelmaking service bureau.

A professional modelmaker assembles an appearance model for the ECOtality Blink range of chargers (see page 30). The material used is a Ren Shape® high-density PU modelling board. Note the additive modelmaking approach.

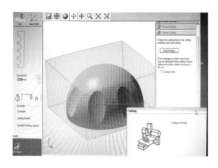

Polyurethane being CNC machined on a desktop CNC milling machine.

Because the materials are easy to cut, they can also be machined with lighter-weight prototyping mills, which are both easier to operate and less costly to run than larger production machines. These smaller mills are suitable for smaller shops and are often used in schools as well.

Gluing

Glue is used to laminate material and to join different pieces together. Foam will often be combined with other materials, and in such cases the glue needs to be compatible with both materials. Also see Chapter 9 on adhesives (page 79).

Glue	PU to PU	PU to Styrene or Acrylic	PU to Metal
Polyurethane Glue	√		
Epoxy	√	√	√
Cyanoacrylate	√	√	√

Filling, Sealing and Painting

Lower-density foams leave visible pores when painted. Higher-density machining boards (480kg/m3 or 30lb/ft3) have a smooth surface that can be primed and painted smooth. The higher-density modelling board is therefore used for high-fidelity appearance models.

Low-density PU foam shows porosity when primed and painted (top row), whereas high-density PU foam is smooth when painted (bottom row).

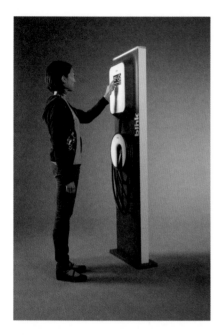

The ECOtality Blink charger model is painted and fitted with screens and other interactive details.

Since the high-density foam is more costly and hard to work by hand, it is sometimes worthwhile to spend the extra energy to smooth the porous low-density foam. This can be done by covering the entire surface either with polyfilla or with several coats of water-based clear polyurethane varnish. A water-based varnish will dry much faster than an oil-based product and does not outgas the same organic solvent fumes. The idea is to build up a clear continuous coating that will seal the pores before painting. Five coats with light sanding in between will produce the best results. This is the same approach that is commonly used to seal wood before painting (see page 137).

The foam density is a factor when selecting fillers. Automotive and epoxy-based fillers are not suitable for low-density foam, since they are harder to sand than their substrates. Water-based acrylic paints are available in a large variety of colours; please refer to Chapter 18 on painting. Please refer to Chapter 9 on adhesives and fillers (page 79) and Chapter 18 on painting (page 154) for additional information.

Detailing

High-quality appearance models will often incorporate other details, including screens, buttons and graphics. It is therefore common for a model to include other materials such as clear plastics, as well as parts made from rapid prototyping processes. Please refer to Chapter 19 on graphics for information on how to produce and apply graphic labels (see page 161).

Tutorial

Game Controller

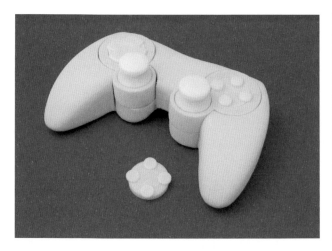

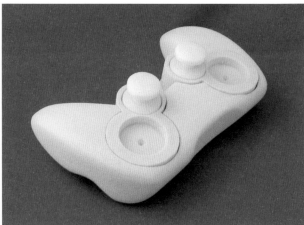

A complex organic form can be difficult to create in 3D CAD. Sometimes it is better made by hand and then scanned in to the program as a guide for surface creation (see Chapter 7 on workflow, page 53). This tutorial shows how a game controller was shaped by hand in low-density PU foam (240kg/m3 or 15lb/ft3). The interactive elements (buttons and paddles) were designed directly in 3D, since they are simple geometric shapes that are easier to computer-model. These were made separately using the Dimension 3D printer.

Overview: The model consists of a complex organic-shaped main housing. Joysticks and buttons sit in protruding cylindrical housings that are distinct from the main form.

Step 1 The process starts with sketching the form of the product. Scale top and side views will be used as cutting templates. These can be hand-drawn or created in Illustrator®.

Step 2 Workflow is planned with some quick sketches. In terms of additive modelling, the main housing, the cylindrical bodies that house the controllers and the buttons will be made as separate pieces and then joined.

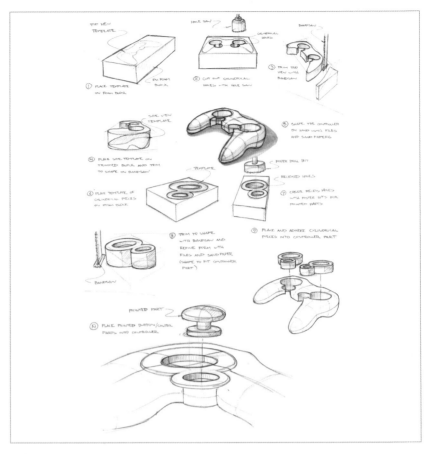

Step 3 The top outline of the game controller is glued on to a piece of PU foam that has been trimmed to the overall thickness. The cylindrical control housing outlines will also be cut from the same piece of foam.

Step 4 Holes are first cut in the main housing to make room for the cylindrical control housings. This can be done with a hole saw mounted on a drill press, or with a scroll saw. Note that power tools require adequate training and supervision.

Step 5 The outlines are now cut with the bandsaw (or a scroll saw).

Step 6 The shaped outline is then sanded smooth and a side-profile template attached. In the process of removing material for the cylindrical pieces, the main housing has become weak and risks breaking when the side profile is sanded.

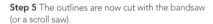

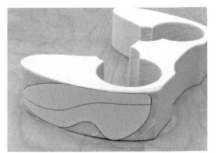

Step 7 The solution is to use a portion of the cylindrical control housings to strengthen the part. The two cylindrical protrusions are cut in half so that the bottom half of each piece can be glued into the main body to create a stronger part. The top halves are saved so that they can be added at the end to create distinct and protruding cylindrical forms.

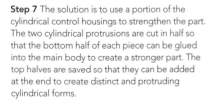

Step 8 The side profile is then sanded to shape on a belt sander. This could have been done with a hand-held rasp instead, in which case the part would be mounted in a vice while being worked on.

 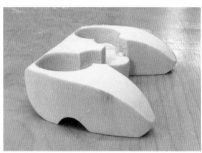

Step 9 The finger-rest concave surface is sanded with a post sander. This could also be done with a circular-shaped rasp.

 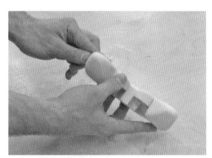

Step 10 The shape is now sanded manually, blending the surfaces into a final desired shape.

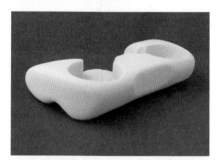 

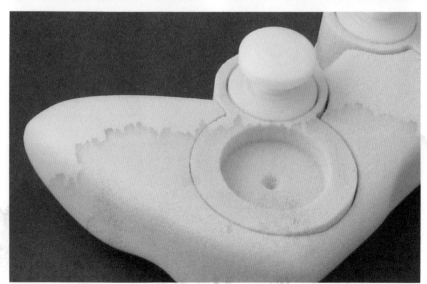

Step 11 The cylindrical protrusions are now glued into place with cyanoacrylate glue. This additive approach shows how important it is to break a form down into its constituent parts and to build each separately.

15

WOOD

Safety Check

— Read Chapter 5 on health and safety
— Obtain professional training and supervision before using power or machine tools
— Wear a dust mask and use a dust-collection system, or vacuum frequently, when sanding
— Some woods are strong sensitizers
— Try to use sheet materials that do not contain formaldehyde

Wood is a common and renewable natural material, a complex and incredibly varied resource that comes in different weights and degrees of stiffness. Trees are confined to their particular climate and environment, but certain varieties of wood are exported widely around the globe for their natural properties. Classified as either softwood or hardwood, wood originates either from evergreen trees, such as spruce, pine and cedar or from deciduous varieties such as cherry, walnut, mahogany and birch. The lightest wood available is Ecuadorian balsawood, widely used to make model aeroplanes.

Softwoods come from needle-bearing evergreen trees (conifers), whereas hardwoods tend to be from broad-leaved deciduous trees. The term hardwood can, however, be misleading; balsa, for example, is very soft, but is technically a hardwood. A more accurate measure of the wood's hardness is therefore density, which varies from 150kg/m3 (10lb/ft3) for balsa to 1,000kg/m3 (60lb/ft3) for ebony.

The term 'wood grain' is often used to describe the colour and texture formed by the annual growth rings of the tree. Oak and walnut have a very noticeable grain, whereas linden (tilia or basswood in North America) has a very fine and consistent light grain. As seen in the pictures below, the grain runs in a vertical direction, alternating between lighter and darker shades. The strength of the wood is also aligned with the fibres that grow in this direction.

Deciduous trees, such as oak (top), are classified as hardwoods, whereas conifers, such as pine (above), are classifed as softwoods.

The grain of the wood is shown in its colour and texture. Linden/basswood (left), red oak (middle) and black walnut (right).

Wood is graded for different applications and markets. Construction timber is likely to be fast-growing softwoods, such as spruce, and is likely to have knots and splits. Furniture-grade wood is selected not to have deficiencies and is also kiln-dried, making it resistant to splitting and shrinking. There is an associated trade-off in cost and availability.

Wood is commonly sold as board or sheet. Veneers are very thin sheets of wood sliced from a board and are applied to finish the surfaces of furniture. Mouldings and round dowels are useful for prototyping projects.

Sheet materials include plywood, chipboard, medium-density fibreboard (MDF) and Masonite. Plywood is made by laminating at least three thin sheets of wood veneer at right angles to each other. This cross-lamination of wood fibres gives the material strength in both directions, enabling it to resist bending and warping. Construction-grade plywood has a rough finish and often shows knots. It is primarily structural and is useful for a variety of applications where strength and low cost is important, for example, to hold something during a test, also known as a test jig. Finer furniture-grade plywood is laminated with a top layer of high-quality hardwood, such as cherry, birch or walnut. Aircraft modelmaking plywood is a very strong, thin sheet material most commonly found in hobby or craft shops. The thickness typically varies from 1mm (0.04in) to 5mm (0.2in), making it suitable for fine-detailed projects such as mechanisms. Flexiply or flexi-plywood is another useful plywood material, which has all the layers of veneer running in the same direction, allowing the board to bend along the grain of the wood. Be careful when planning though, as the flexi-plywood will bend only in this one direction.

Wood is sold in many forms, including board, sheet, mouldings, dowels and veneer.

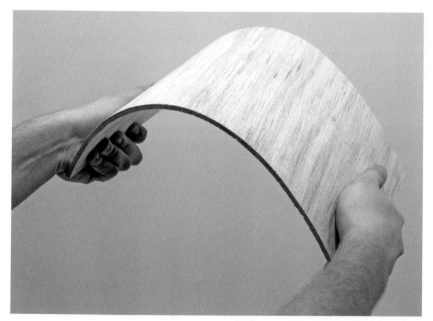

Plywood (above) is made in different grades for different applications. Bendy or flexi-plywood (left) is a useful material for creating curved planes in wood.

Case Study Leaning Clothes Rack in Flexi-Plywood

This case study by Dennis Cheng (Carleton University, Ottawa) shows how it is possible to be creative with process. Curved plywood, as popularized by Charles and Ray Eames in the 1950s, is produced in industry by custom-moulding plywood. The most expedient way to prototype this is by using flexi-plywood.

The curved sections were achieved by laminating two separate sheets of flexi-plywood together with glue. When the glue sets the resulting shear holds the curved shape.

The clothes-rack design called for a fairly tight radius on the top edge of the rack where it transitions from front to back. This had a functional and visual purpose but presented a prototyping challenge, as it was impossible to bend the flexi-plywood that tightly. Using the approach of additive modelling, a separate curved front and back section were instead created and then joined with a solid wooden block spacer that had been shaped to include the top radius. A thin sheet of high-quality wood veneer was finally laminated to the outside surface, creating the illusion of a single curved sheet of ply running from the front to the back, which clothes could be draped over.

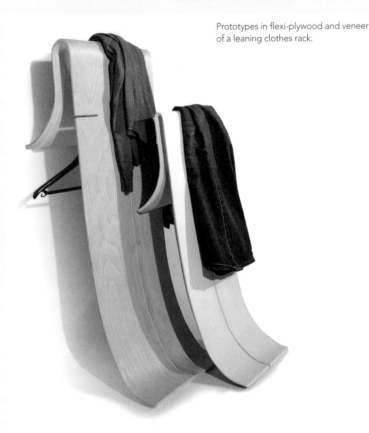

Prototypes in flexi-plywood and veneer of a leaning clothes rack.

Clamps hold two pieces of flexi-plywood together during the lamination process.

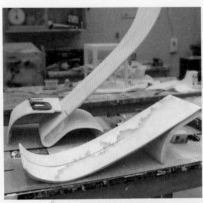

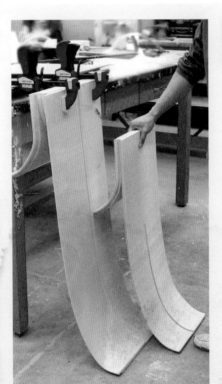

Using flexi-plywood and an additive approach, three separate pieces were joined, creating an illusion of a single flowing wooden sheet.

Applications for Wood

Good strength, ease of handling and low cost are features that make wood an attractive material for an immense variety of low- as well as high-fidelity prototyping applications. One of the primary uses of wood is in furniture projects. Standard joinery and woodworking methods are beyond the scope of this book, as the focus here is not on fine woodworking. The focus is instead on effective and practical means by which to achieve a desired result.

Wood is also used in a variety of ways beyond furniture. Vacuum-forming moulds are typically made from wood. These can be made with traditional tools or, if the facilities exist, CNC-machined pieces.

Preparing a vacuum-forming tool out of wood.

Explorative Prototypes

Fiskars is famous for its wide range of well-designed and innovative hand tools. Dan Lipscomb, who works at Fiskars, uses plywood, among other materials, to explore new ideas for products. A new cultivator product was prototyped with plywood and dowels, in order to produce a sufficiently rigid model to demonstrate the idea to his colleagues. In this case the prototype focused solely on function, as it was simply an explorative proof of concept. Aircraft plywood would be suitable for such a project.

Appearance Prototypes for Communication

Wood is also used for appearance models, especially larger projects where material costs are a particular concern, or when the designer wishes to use more natural and environmentally-friendly choices. Wood varieties such as linden (basswood) are particularly useful since they have very little grain and are easy not only to sand and carve, but also to finish and paint to simulate other materials, such as plastic. There is more work involved than when using polyurethane modelling board, since the surface needs many layers of sealant to completely cover the wood grain, but new fast-drying water-based polyurethane sealers will speed up the process.

This electric chainsaw student project illustrates how the same wood (linden, or basswood) was used to create both a low-fidelity ergonomic user-testing model and the high-fidelity appearance model shown on the right.

Designer Dan Lipscomb at Fiskars constructed a works-like prototype in plywood for a cultivator mechanism.

The versatility of wood is illustrated in this student project for a new electric chainsaw design. Linden (basswood) was used for both the low-fidelity test model (left) and the final high-fidelity appearance prototype (right).

Laminating pieces of linden for a large vacuum-forming mould.

Working with Wood

There are many factors to consider when choosing wood, including strength, toughness, weight, appearance and cost. This is why it is important to consider the application carefully. Is it an early low-fidelity prototype or a high-fidelity appearance prototype? Will the model be painted?

Eye protection and dust masks are essential in woodworking. Power tools should never be used without proper training and supervision.

Preparation

Planning is essential. Sometimes the required workpiece is larger than the boards of wood available. This means that the wood needs to be laminated into thicker sections with glue.

Cutting

The bandsaw is probably the most versatile and common saw for modelmaking applications (see page 61). The scroll saw is also a good tool for intricate outlines and for creating interior openings. Larger wood shops have a range of other equipment, including table and mitre saws, to produce more accurate straight cuts. Outlines in wood are usually cut using a paper template as a cutting outline. A little bit of extra material is left on the workpiece for subsequent finishing.

A scroll-saw blade can be inserted in a drilled access hole to cut out an interior opening, as shown in this tool handle example. As before, leave 1mm (0.04in) of clearance between the paper template and the saw blade for subsequent finishing.

A paper template is useful as a cutting guide. The bandsaw is used for exterior cuts, whereas interior openings are created by drilling an access hole for the jigsaw or scroll saw. Make sure to leave a millimetre of extra material for subsequent finishing.

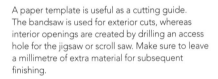

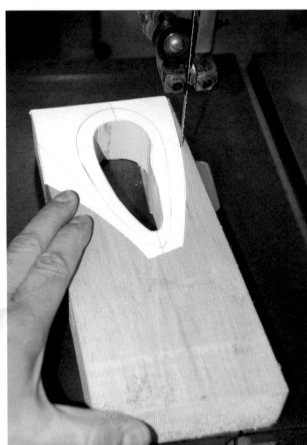

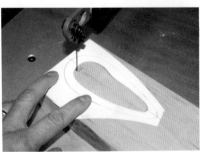

Shaping

Wood can be carved into intricate shapes. Some traditional hand-tool methods are very effective and useful. The approach to an effective manual workflow is:

1. Cut the wood leaving a bit of material for finishing
2. Rough out the shape
3. Smooth the shape

The rasp is an effective hand tool that removes a lot of material quickly. It is important to use a good solid vice, since this is the only way to provide sufficient support. A flat rasp is used for outside surfaces and a round rasp for the inside curved surfaces.

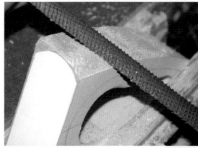

The rasp is a fast and effective tool for rough shaping. Pieces should be clamped securely. A round rasp will work better on inside corners, as shown on the handle opening below left.

Once the shape has been roughed in, it is time to move to sandpaper, starting with a coarse 80-grit paper and progressing toward finer grades (120, 240 grit).

Final smoothing uses progressively finer grades of sandpaper.

Power tools are frequently used to work with wood, but require professional training and supervision. Dust collection is essential to minimize the amount of airborne dust. The disc sander and post sander are used to sand convex and concave shapes respectively. The approach is to leave some margin when the initial cutting is done so that the final shape can be sanded to a more accurate and smooth finish.

Disc sanders and post sanders can be used to fine-tune a cut outline.

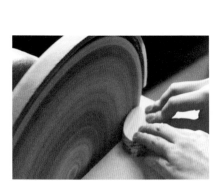

The wooden lathe is used to make more than wooden bowls. Circular wooden shapes can be combined with other parts through additive modelling.

CNC machining is increasingly accessible in schools as well as industry. The CNC is programmed first to do a roughing operation with a larger cutter to remove as much material as possible. This is followed by finer mill cutters that remove smaller but more exact amounts of materials before the final sanding coat. See Chapter 8 on CNC machining and laser cutting (page 74).

This wave-like texture was created in Rhinoceros® and milled on a three-axis CNC router. The surface texture left by the ball end mill is visible and would need to be manually sanded to get a perfectly smooth texture.

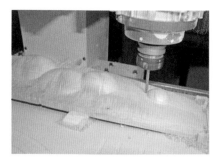

Far left: The bottom of an asymmetric wooden bowl is machined on a CNC mill using geometry from Rhinoceros®.

Left: The top of a wooden bowl CNC machined by master cabinetmaker Randy Kerr.

Filling, Sealing and Painting

Water-based wood fillers have come a long way and are less noxious than their solvent-based counterparts. The fillers come in many colours, and if the wood is to be stained it is advisable to test first, as the filler may absorb less stain than the wood and thus appear lighter or darker.

If wood is used to simulate other materials such as plastics, then the pores and grain in the wood need to be sealed before the model can be painted. A minimum of five layers is required to conceal the wood grain. Water-based polyurethane dries quickly between coats (15 minutes). It can be sanded with medium to fine sandpaper between applications. Feel the surface for imperfections or texture. The part should feel smooth before priming.

Wood fillers are required to fill cracks or fix surface blemishes.

Sealing wood with several layers of water-based polyurethane ensures that the wood grain is hidden when painting.

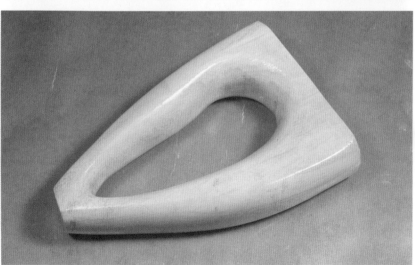

MODELLING CLAY

Safety Check

— Read Chapter 5 on health and safety
— Heat lamps and ovens present a fire hazard
— Read SDS information

Various different types of clay are used in product design. Clay is a naturally expressive and sculptural medium, easily manipulated by hand and simple tools. For complex and organic forms it is often the modelmaking material of choice.

Clay is often the material of choice to develop highly complex organic forms, such as this helmet by Alan Okamura for the Spanish bicycle-gear company Spiuk. The helmet clay model was made using styling clay, which can also be painted.

Types of Clay

Plasticine Clay

Plasticine is helpful for quickly and effectively examining formal aspects while sketching. As it stays soft and pliable it cannot hold detail and is useful only for temporary work. It is also used as a complement to modify polystyrene models.

Polymer Clay

Polymer clays are modern craft materials sold in various colours and finishes with brand names such as Fimo® or Sculpey®. They are soft and easily shaped, but turn hard when baked. After this heat curing they can then be sanded, drilled and painted, making them quite versatile for modelmaking. They are also suitable for smaller projects such as figurines, action figures and jewellery.

Plasticine is useful for quick form studies and even helps visualization while sketching (far left). It can also be applied on top of foam models to look at formal variations, as shown in the early form models for Tana Water (left).

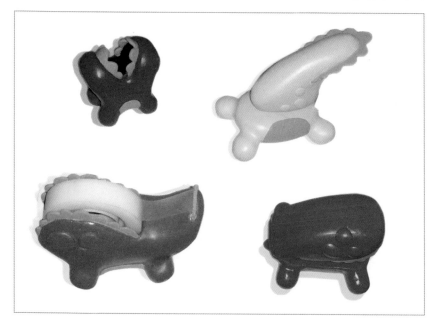

Polymer clay is available in various colours and hardens when baked. Small, detailed parts, such as this series of children's stationery items (tape dispenser, stapler), can be easily modelled by hand in polymer clay.

Styling Clay

Popularized by Harley Earl at General Motors in the 1950s, styling clay has become the de facto physical modelling material in transport design. It is well suited to developing large flowing surfaces and complex sculptural transitions. The automotive styling clays are formulated with wax to be hard at room temperature but turn soft when heated. This dual state is extremely useful and versatile, since these clays can easily be worked by hand while warm, while being able to be carved in detail when cooled. What is particularly interesting is how modern car design in clay really exemplifies the convergence of digital and traditional workflow. Clay models will be initiated from 2D sketches. The finished models are then scanned into 3D and manipulated further. Finally, full-scale clay models are milled on giant five-axis machines. Designers can then tweak the machined model and restart the iterative process.

Case Study Olme Spyder

Working from hand drawings and rendering, the students first developed different quarter-scale models.

The chosen design direction was scanned in to the computer utilizing a hand-held scanner. The small targets on the model are used by the scanner for alignment. Note how only half the model is required, because of the symmetrical shape.

The Olme Spyder was created over a ten-week period by Masters students in the Transportation Design Programme at Umeå Institute of Design, Sweden. Styling-clay models were first developed at quarter scale. The chosen design direction was then scanned into 3D CAD and developed further into a full-scale CNC-machined polystyrene model.

The ability to scan handmade models into 3D space exemplifies a new type of workflow that integrates analogue and digital models in a seamless fashion, but also underscores the importance of learning through working with one's hands.

The scanned-in data served as a guide for surface development in 3D CAD using Alias software. This data was used to create highly photorealistic renderings, as shown above.

A large five-axis Kolb CNC machine was used to mill a full-scale model out of a large block of polystyrene foam.

Product Design Clay

In product design programmes, the skill of working in clay has not been taught at the same level as in automotive design programmes, but its role is expanding as new, easier-to-work formulations become available. New digital workflow, such as the ability to scan clay models into 3D CAD, is an important incentive to use the material as an analogue input device.

Product design styling clay is about 40 per cent lighter than the traditional automotive clays and does not have their unpleasant odour derived from sulphur fillers. They work in the same way, in that they become soft and pliable when heated, and turn hard when cooled for carving.

Kolb Technologies of Germany has developed InDeClay in response to the needs of product designers. This clay has a grey colour that the manufacturer claims shows shadows better. It is also virtually odour-free. The tutorial at the end of this chapter uses this material. The North American company Chavant also offers a product design sulphur-free clay product. These materials differ in hardness and feel, making it a matter of personal preference which is chosen.

Working with Styling Clay

Whereas plasticine and polymer clays are basically worked by hand, there are some more elaborate tricks and tools necessary for working with styling clay. First and foremost, styling-clay models are rarely made solely from clay. They tend to be built on top of a simple armature that both supports the clay and reduces the amount of clay material. A Styrofoam armature is often used (see tutorial on page 143).

Softening Clay with Heat

Before clay is applied it has to be softened with heat. Typically, the clays can be heated to a temperature of 55°C (130°F). The softened clay is added to the armature by hand into an approximate shape and carved once it cools to room temperature. Care should be taken to not overheat the clay as this will destroy the material. An electric chafing dish, normally used to heat food, is a suitable heating source, as it will keep the clay warm without overheating it.

Tools

Once the clay has cooled to room temperature it can be carved in intricate detail. Different tools are used to accomplish different tasks. These tools progress in function from the coarse removal of material to the creation of finer levels of detail.

Kolb InDeClay and Chavant Y2K styling clays are suitable for larger-scale projects such as helmets. See page 143.

Clay billets are usually cut into smaller parts and softened in an electric chafing dish. Make sure to keep temperature at or below the manufacturer's suggested temperature.

Rakes are used initially to remove a significant amount of material so as to establish an overall shape. They often have teeth in order to be more effective.

Wire tools are useful for carving finer details. Professional tools are precision-cut from thin sheet metal with accurate ground-cutting surfaces. They come in a variety of shapes.

Finishers are used to create an even surface by scraping thinner amounts of clay.

Slicks, made from thin spring steel, are used for final finishing.

A basic toolset from Kolb, including a 75mm (3in) curved rake, 30mm (1.2in) finisher, three wire tools and a 0.2mm (0.008in) thick spring-steel slick, is sufficient as a starting point.

Since many of these tools have been specifically developed for larger automotive applications, not all of them are required for smaller projects. Since the tools are expensive it is worth noting that a basic set of tools will be able to accomplish the majority of projects. Students may even wish to make their own tools.

Tapes

One of the most useful techniques is to use paper tape to create edges and transitions. The tapes are used both when adding and when subtracting material. The tape works as a mask for the tool, as it will not cut as easily through the tape as the clay. This allows the edge of the tape to act as a guide for sharp and defined surface transitions. The preferred tapes are made from rice paper and can be ordered directly from the clay manufacturer. They come in various thicknesses and are easy both to cut and to curve along the surface.

Painting and Finishing

When a clay model is built to study form, it is not usually necessary to paint the model, but if required these clays do have the added advantage of being paintable. Primers and fillers can be used directly on top of the clay in order to attain a high-level finish.

Rice-paper tapes are used as guides to define edges and surface transitions when carving the clay with a finisher or set of slicks. Tape is used to define concave as well as protruding surfaces.

Tutorial · Clay Helmet

The following conceptual helmet tutorial shows some of the advantages and techniques of working with clay. The helmet is built on top of a mannequin head, which also serves as an armature for the prototype. This model is only a 3D sketch and does not reflect accurate helmet dimensions. To save time only half the helmet is modelled. Inserting a mirror on the plane of symmetry can in essence check the full effect. Also note that the visor has not been modelled in the exercise.

Planning The helmet was drawn with freehand sketches. These are not to scale and work only as a visual guide for the 3D clay model. When it comes to complex 3D shapes such as helmets, a 3D model will add more to our understanding of the form beyond what the sketches often visualize.

Step 1 The tutorial was made with Kolb's InDeClay and a set of basic tools (far left). The armature is a standard Styrofoam mannequin head (below), and tape is used to define the profile of the helmet. A suitable oven or heat lamp is required to soften the clay billet to 55°C (130°F).

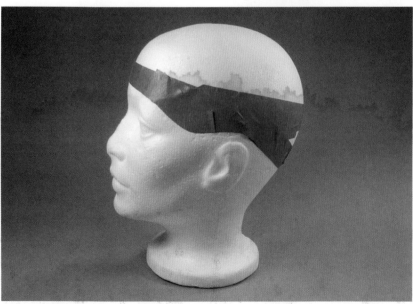

Step 2 Clay is added until an approximate shape is realized. A Styrofoam base is added to the head form to improve stability on the top-heavy model.

Step 3 The helmet shape is initially carved with a toothed rake that removes effective amounts of clay. Typically, this also reveals low spots that have to be filled with more clay. It is advisable first to heat the model slightly in order to improve adhesion of the new layer of clay.

Step 4 Tape is used in order to create a sharp transition at the parting line. Normally rice-paper tape would be used, but in this case simple masking tape was used to show that it can act as a substitute. A finisher is used to shave the clay to an even surface, worked in different directions in order to get a more consistent finish.

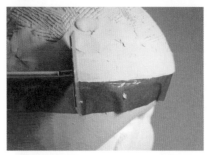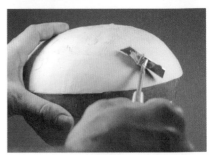

Step 5 The top surface is finally slicked with a 0.2mm (0.008in) thick spring-steel slick. It is important to work in different directions with the slick in order not to establish a low spot.

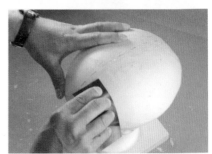

Step 6 The concave side-ventilation opening is added. The ventilation features will be added only to one side of the helmet. Tape is used to define the edge, and various tools are used to remove material to the desired shape.

Step 7 The top vent depression is a bit more complicated and requires a two-step process. First, rice-paper tape is used to define the edge of the surface depression. This depression is then carved out to the desired depth.

Step 8 Tape is added on the inside edge that delineates the surface chamfer. Clay can now be added safely without destroying the previously refined surfaces, and scraped back to the predefined tape edges. This shows how tape can be used for adding precise feature transitions.

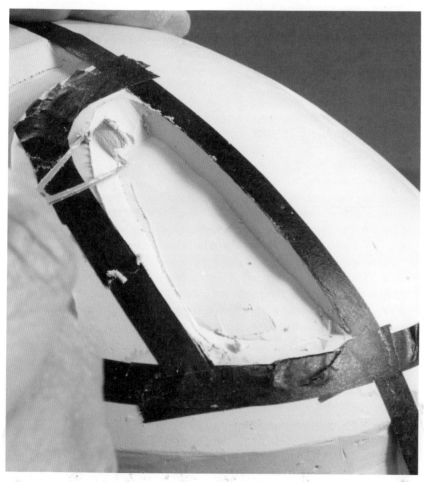

Step 9 The final ventilation surfaces are added in the same manner, using tape to define edges and protect existing surfaces. Note how only half the helmet is detailed in order to avoid issues of symmetry and to save time.

CASTING

Safety Check

— Read Chapter 5 on health and safety
— With uncured chemicals, work only in well-ventilated areas such as a spray booth or fume hood
— Prevent skin contact with chemicals by wearing suitable clothing and rubber gloves
— Read SDS information

Casting involves pouring a liquid polymer into a mould in order to make parts. A two-part material is mixed together just before pouring so that it can set inside the mould. Some parts are more easily cast than others. Thin-walled and complex parts are more demanding than thicker, flatter pieces. In industry, professional designers will usually outsource a casting job, as it tends to require a lot of experience and specialized equipment to get perfect parts. Students who wish to experiment with mixing materials and mould construction in order to gain an understanding of the casting process should know that not all mould materials are created equal. There is a wide variety of materials for mouldmaking and it is extremely important to use the safer materials sold for home or hobby use rather than industrial materials intended for production. Read the instructions and supplied Safety Data Sheets (for both parts) carefully for your own protection against toxic chemicals. Also follow the manufacturer's instructions about mixing or else the material may not set properly. Once the materials have set, they can be handled like other materials.

DW Product Development used casting to produce small numbers of the SureClose compost bin. This was helpful in verifying many design aspects before injection-mould tooling. The high-quality castings are visually and functionally equivalent to production parts, capturing fine details such as the debossed city logo, as well as the fine mesh of ventilation openings. These parts were outsourced to a company specializing in casting.

Applications for Casting

Small-Volume Production

In small-volume quantities casting provides a fast and cost-effective alternative to mass-production tooling. Casting can produce very strong and resilient parts that are virtually identical to production parts, but without substantial tooling investment. These parts can be used in field trials and when multiples are required for marketing efforts. This allows the design team to obtain feedback and the marketing team to work with clients before product delivery. Thin-walled and accurate parts such as the SureClose compost bin shown above left, require highly specialized casting expertise and equipment and are best outsourced to professional modelmakers or casting companies.

Rubber can be cast in a wide variety of stiffnesses, colours and levels of transparency, as shown in these Silicone samples from Smooth-On, Inc.

Elastomeric Parts

Elastomeric (rubber-like) parts are usually made through the casting process, although new developments in rapid prototyping are increasingly able to do this as well. Silicone and polyurethane rubber can be cast in a variety of stiffnesses and colours. Even clear and translucent parts can be cast in rubber. The durometer reading is a measure of the rubber stiffness, or hardness. For example, a very soft gelatinous material might have a reading of 10 on the Shore A durometer scale, whereas a bicycle inner tube would have a reading of approximately 50 Shore A.

Reproduction in Harder Material

A model made in clay or foam is very fragile. The model can, however, be used to make a mould so that a harder material can be used to make castings.

Clear Parts

Prototyping clear parts through the casting process is an alternative to machining parts out of solid stock. Building clear parts through an additive modelmaking process is not possible, since the glues and fillers will be visible. A model made in such a way can still be made to produce patterns for casting. The main challenge with casting crystal-clear parts is to remove air bubbles, and some of these materials require extra safety protection.

Casting Process

In order to understand casting one needs to become familiar with some of the basic components of a mould and how it is made.

Pattern

The pattern is the part that is to be cast. For the purposes of modelmaking we will assume that the pattern is a model made by the designer. Some materials used for mouldmaking or casting will shrink as they set, in which case this has to be accounted for by using a scaled-up pattern incorporating the shrinkage. Patterns can be made in most materials, but if made in styling clay, the clay must be of a sulphur-free variety so as not to inhibit the mould setting process. Patterns also have to be clean and free of grease or silicone for the same reason. The pattern is usually finished to a high level before making the mould, since this saves time in terms of finishing each cast part.

Mould

Mouldmaking silicones are two-part compounds that are mixed together and poured over the pattern until they set. The silicone will capture the finest details on the pattern and is flexible, so that minor undercuts do not present a problem.

The easiest mould to make is a one-part mould. This type of mould can be made if the part can be open-cast and if it is fairly solid. If the bottom of the part is flat, then the silicone is cast on top of the pattern and is then peeled off once it has set. The resulting mould is then turned over so that casting compound can be poured into the bottom opening. A mould box is required to retain the silicone while it sets.

First, two-part liquid silicone is poured over the pattern in a mould box. Once hardened and removed, the resulting silicone mould captures all the details of the pattern.

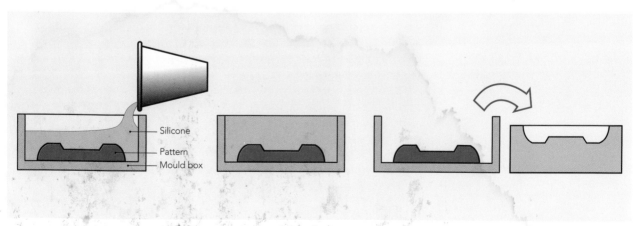

Silicone
Pattern
Mould box

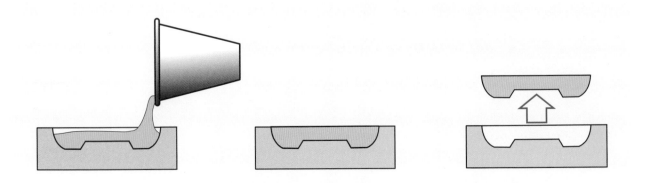

Next, the mould is used to cast two-part liquid plastic. The part is removed from the mould after it has set.

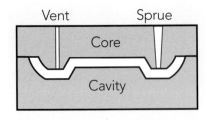

Two-part moulds need a sprue to pour liquid casting material into, and vents to allow air to escape.

When the part has two sides, then a two-part mould is necessary. Imagine the part above, but with a uniform wall thickness. Two-sided moulds consist of a core to define the back or inside of the part and a cavity to define the front or outside of the part.

In order to pour casting resin into the two-sided mould, additional features need to be added to allow material to flow in and to allow air to escape. The sprue is the opening into which the casting material is poured. The sprue is left full when pouring to ensure that the mould fills completely. Air also needs to be able to leave the mould via vents. These features can be added to the pattern while pouring the mould, or by cutting away channels in the silicone mould afterwards.

The simplest method to make such a mould is to encapsulate the part and then cut the mould into two separate parts. When the mould is cut apart you need to take care not to damage the pattern or the mould. This presents some inherent issues of quality. It is essentially a quick and dirty approach.

A better approach is to create the two separate halves in two distinct steps. A common technique is to use plasticine to create a temporary mould half in a mould box. By mounting the pattern in plasticine, with only half the pattern protruding, it is possible to define the parting line. Silicone is then poured on top, resulting in a second mould half. The temporary plasticine is then removed and the process repeated in reverse to create the remaining half in silicone.

Casting Materials

Hard plastic parts are cast in polyurethane resins. These are two-part components that are mixed together in an exothermic reaction. Home or hobby varieties that do not require degassing equipment are less likely to leave air bubbles in the parts. Many different materials exist with different material properties. The heat deflection temperature (HDT) is an important measure of the temperature at which the cast part can operate after it has set and hardened. If the HDT is 50°C (122°F) then the casting will start deforming at temperatures that exceed this, which can easily happen in the sun or the boot of a car. Some resins are clear and can be tinted to various translucent colours; others are opaque white and can be tinted to various opaque colours. Polyurethane can also be drilled, sanded and painted after casting.

Rubber-like parts are cast in silicone or polyurethane rubber. Some of the materials used to make moulds are also used to make parts. Opaque and clear formulations can be tinted to custom colour, which is important because rubber parts cannot be finished or painted.

Since the parts are made from rubber and are flexible, it means that the moulds can in fact be hard. They could, for example, be CNC machined or made by rapid prototyping.

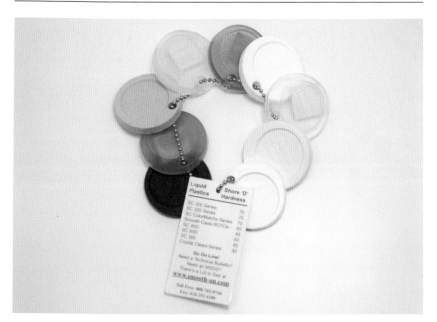

Polyurethane can be cast in a number of colours, and with a variety of structural properties and degrees of clarity as shown in these samples from Smooth-On, Inc.

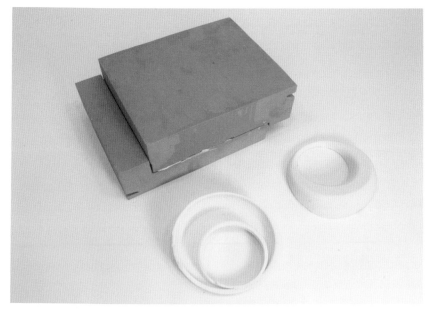

Silicone parts are flexible and can be cast in solid CNC-machined moulds. The flash (excess material) on the moulded part is trimmed away with a scalpel after the part has set.

Case Study Casting Comic Figures

This two-sided mould in silicone rubber was used for the purpose of small production of a comic figure designed by Teddy Luong (Carleton University, Ottawa). The figurine was created in Rhinoceros® 3D CAD software. The pattern was rapid prototyped and finished smooth with sanding, filler and primer. The mould was made in 40 Shore A durometer silicone rubber by first encapsulating half the pattern in plasticine clay in a simple mould box made from Lego®.

A mould box made from Lego® is used to cast a figure. The first step is to define the parting line by creating a temporary mould core using plasticine. The plasticine defines the parting line and includes dome-shaped registration features.

Silicone is mixed and poured into the mould box on top of the plasticine-encapsulated figurine. This created the front half of the silicone mould.

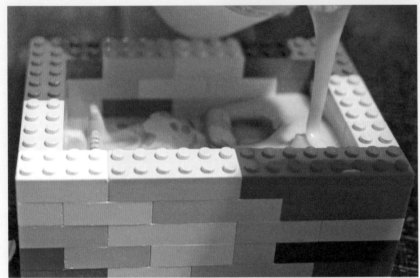

When the silicone had set, the plasticine was discarded. The back half of the mould could now be created in reverse on top of the front half. The completed two-part mould is shown on the right. The mould will be filled through the bottom of the figurine's feet, which will act as both sprue and vent.

Multiple characters are moulded in polyurethane casting plastic and are then custom-painted.

Case Study Elastomeric Wristband

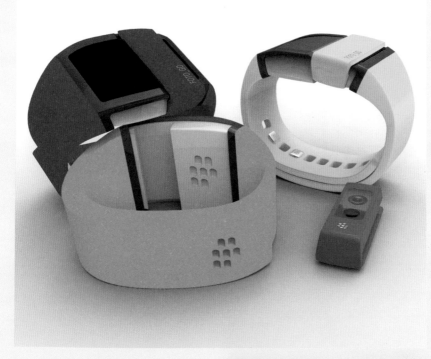

Designed by Marc Boycott (Carleton University, Ottawa), the Foto-Go is a wearable lifestyle camera that captures personal events and interactions in an ongoing fashion.

For prototyping the camera, silicone wristbands were cast in various colours, using a mould. The mould could technically have been hard, since the silicone parts are flexible, but given the complex geometry and parting line it would have been difficult to design and machine such a mould. A hard pattern was therefore made instead using rapid prototyping, which in turn was used to make a silicone mould. The pattern was sanded, filled and primed to a very smooth finish before casting. Note how all material mixing and pouring was done in the spray booth. The mould was left there until it set.

Materials are gathered for mouldmaking. The wristband pattern is a rapid prototype that has been finished to a high level of fidelity through sanding, filling and painting.

The wristband has a curved parting line. A temporary plasticine mould base is created that positions the pattern to minimize undercuts in the mould. Styrene sheets are hot-glued together to create the mould base. Oversized styrene sheets can be used to make different-sized moulds by simply overlapping the sheets as shown. The wooden pegs are used as alignment pins (not strictly necessary).

A spray-on mould release is applied. This helps in the removal of the pattern at the end.

Silicone parts A and B are carefully measured and mixed together thoroughly to the manufacturer's instructions. Note how disposable gloves are worn when mixing and pouring materials.

The first half of the mould is now poured, starting in a corner so as not to trap air bubbles.

When the material has set, the mould is disassembled and the plasticine discarded.

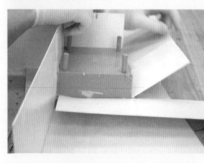 

The process is now repeated in reverse. Note that small plasticine shapes have been added to the patterns in order to create the sprue and vent on each part.

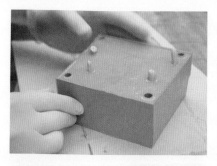

The mould is now complete. Note the sprue and vent openings on the part.

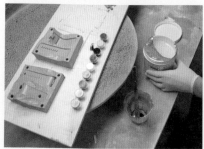

The mould is now ready for casting silicone wristbands. Clear silicone is mixed with custom colourants.

The silicone is injected into the mould with a syringe. The mould is filled through the sprue until the mould is full and material exits at the vent.

After the silicone sets, the mould is taken apart to free the parts. Flash at the parting line is trimmed off carefully afterwards.

The same mould is used to cast a variety of wristbands in different colours.

PAINTING: MORE THAN AN AFTERTHOUGHT

Safety Check

— Read Chapter 5 on health and safety
— Preferably use water-based paints
— Spray paint only in ventilated areas such as a spray booth or outside
— Prevent skin contact by wearing suitable clothing and rubber gloves
— Read SDS information

The decision regarding when and how to paint is dependent on the purpose of the prototype. A highly finished model that is intended to have the exact appearance of the final product will require substantial attention to painting technique and colour selection, whereas earlier models may simply be painted in a grey or white neutral primer to hide fillers and glue marks. Painting is more than an afterthought: it is a critical aspect of the design process.

The final model of this hand drill (right) pays special attention to painting technique. Earlier prototyping includes unpainted models and a foam model painted in a neutral grey.

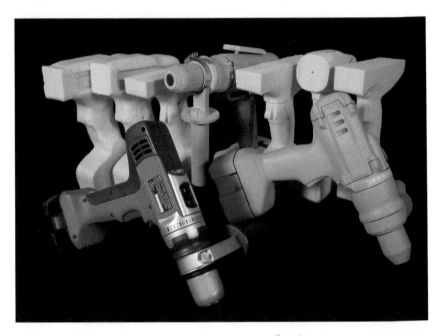

The Pantone Matching System® allows designers to select and specify colour by standard.

Colour

Careful studies of colour generally precede the final paint application. The Pantone Matching System® (PMS) allows designers to pick standard colours that can be matched by paint suppliers and even plastic injection moulders. Graphic design programs can also be used to examine Pantone® colours. It is important to realize that the colour will appear differently depending on the computer monitor. Students should experiment with mixing their own colours as part of their learning.

Since colour appears different in different types of light, it is important to view the colour in the environment of use. A product painted indoors under artificial lighting will look different outside. A paint sample can be created and viewed in the proper light first. There are even special light boxes that are designed with various types of light in them to see the effect on colour.

 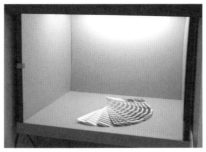 

Above is an illumination box with different types of light to show the effect on colour selection: fluorescent (left), daylight (middle) and incandescent (right).

Texture

Manufactured parts are often painted in a texture in order to reduce the shine and to hide surface imperfections. Many injection-moulded parts are moulded in textures such as MoldTech® textures. Large metal panels are also often painted in a texture to hide manufacturing imperfections. Spray painting can approximate these textures as described in the spray-painting techniques part of the chapter (see page 158).

Gloss, Matt or Metallic

Gloss paint creates a shine and depth that has intense highlights. The problem with a glossy surface is that it shows any small surface imperfections, most notably along highlights. Semi-gloss still has a high shine, but is more forgiving.

Matt is a toned-down version of gloss with a more even reflection that helps mask the imperfections. Even flatter (less glossy) paint will appear as chalkboard and will further hide imperfections. Primers are flat and designed to allow the topcoat to adhere.

The shine can be manipulated to simulate different effects. A gloss or semi-gloss paint (with or without a texture) will appear as injection-moulded ABS, whereas a matt to flat paint will have the appearance of rubber. Metallic paints will create a range of metallic effects, including aluminium and the coloured metallic paint finishes seen on cars.

Types of Paint

For spray painting, waterborne acrylics are the common sense choice. They are available in a wide range of sheens, colours and metallic finishes. Traditional solvent-based lacquers and enamel paints should generally be avoided for environmental reasons.

High-quality artist's supply water-based acrylic paints come in many colours and can be custom-mixed to PMS colour. Airbrush medium is used to dilute the paint for airbrushing (see page 157). Gesso is a thick primer that can be used to paint Styrofoam models.

Although solvent-based lacquers have been popular for their high sheen (gloss) and use in automotive painting, they need solvents for preparation, thinning and clean-up, and this solvent eventually needs to be disposed of in accordance with strict environmental controls. Enamels have similar problems and also take a very long time to dry. Water-based acrylics have simply advanced so much that it seems unnecessary to use anything but these safer, water-clean-up materials. Latex water-based paints and gesso can be used for foam models.

Preparation

Preparation is the most important factor in a high-quality paint job. A good base is a surface that is primed to look and feel uniform. If the surface has not been

A foam brush is used to apply a coat of primer to clean up a foam model (top). Fine sable-hair brushes are used to touch up paint jobs (above).

properly prepared, paint will only make it look worse. Most models will require substantial finishing before the model is ready for paint. This requires filling, priming and sanding surfaces until they are uniformly smooth. It is much easier to paint parts separately before assembly, rather than assemble them and then try to mask the joint line. It is also important not to have any grease or dirt on the parts prior to painting so as to ensure adhesion.

Application

Paint is ideally applied by brush, airbrush or spraygun. Whereas spray cans are popular because of their cost and availability they are, however, hard to control, limited in colour and are not environmentally friendly.

Brushes

Foam brushes are useful for cleaning up messy foam models with a coat of primer or gesso paint. Since these are low-fidelity models, the paint job does not need to be as detailed. Brushes do, however, leave brush marks. Fine brushes are used for detailing and touch-up work.

Spray Painting

Spray painting works by using a compressor or compressed-air tank to force air through a nozzle that then draws paint from a reservoir and atomizes it into a paint stream. Spray painting should be done only in well-ventilated areas, even when using water-based acrylics, as the small particles that are released present a health hazard if inhaled. A professional spray booth is ideal, or smaller compact spray booths can be purchased from the suppliers of airbrush art supplies. These smaller booths are meant solely for artist and hobbyist paints. Respirators provide additional protection, but it is very important to have a health check (see page 49), as well as make sure that the right respirator is chosen and worn properly. Students should be aware of their own school policies before wearing a respirator.

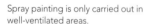

Spray painting is only carried out in well-ventilated areas.

The compressor is what provides the air stream to the airbrush or airgun. A good compressor has an air-pressure tank that regulates the air pressure, as well as a pressure valve and a moisture trap to capture water droplets before they enter the airstream. The compressor will be adjusted somewhere between 20 and 40PSI. A flexible hose is then connected to the sprayer.

The paint has to be diluted to a low enough viscosity to be able to be pulled through the nozzle. This is a function of the paint, pressure, airbrush construction and nozzle opening size. More pressure is needed for thicker paint and smaller nozzle openings. The paint needs to be diluted in order to flow through the airbrush. It is critical to keep the sprayers clean. For water-based acrylics you can use water or water-based airbrush medium to dilute the paint. Start with 25 per cent and then dilute until satisfactory flow and paint application is established.

There are two kinds of airbrushes. The simplest is the single-action airbrush, which only has control of the amount of air going through the nozzle. A dual-action airbrush mixes the paint internally and can control both the airflow and the amount of paint. These are more expensive and harder to clean than single-action airbrushes, but can be used to create special effects such as gradients.

A good compressor has a built-in pressure tank with a regulator and pressure gauge. The water trap below the gauge prevents moisture from entering the air stream. A flexible air hose is connected between the compressor and the sprayer.

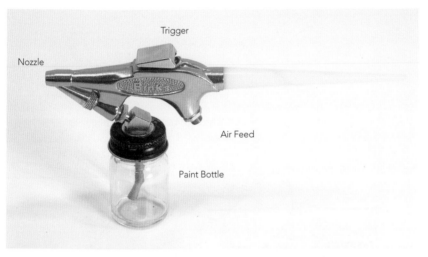

Trigger

Nozzle

Air Feed

Paint Bottle

A single-action airbrush only has a single trigger action, to control airflow. It is easy to use and clean.

A dual-action airbrush has a trigger that can be pushed down (far left) to supply air pressure and rocked backwards (left) to control the amount of paint. This type of airbrush can be used to create gradients while painting, but requires more technique and cleaning.

The airbrush should be cleaned after each paint application. Before the airbrush is put away, it is disassembled and thoroughly cleaned according to manufacturer's instructions.

Paint guns are suitable for larger models and are heavier to hold than an airbrush, so that control is not as fine and delicate. They can usually be adjusted to produce a round paint stream or a narrow paint stream, depending on the painting application. The paint has to be diluted just as in the airbrush.

Spray-Painting Techniques

The key to obtaining a good paint finish is to paint evenly and in thin layers. The model is always primed first. Two to three coats of primer are normal and the paint has to have time to dry to the touch in between coats. Successive coats of paint follow this. The airbrush or paint gun is moved across the model in even, overlapping strokes. The trigger is activated before the stream hits the model and then it is deactivated after the stream leaves the model. This action is repeated back and forth. Practise on a piece of scrap until the technique is learnt. It is also important to work in a clean environment free of dust.

Texture painting requires some practice and experimentation. The basic approach is to paint the part with a uniform coat of paint first. The pressure is then reduced and painting distance increased to achieve a second layer of droplets on top of the original layer. The texture will be a factor of droplet size.

Paint guns are more suitable for painting larger surfaces as they hold more paint.

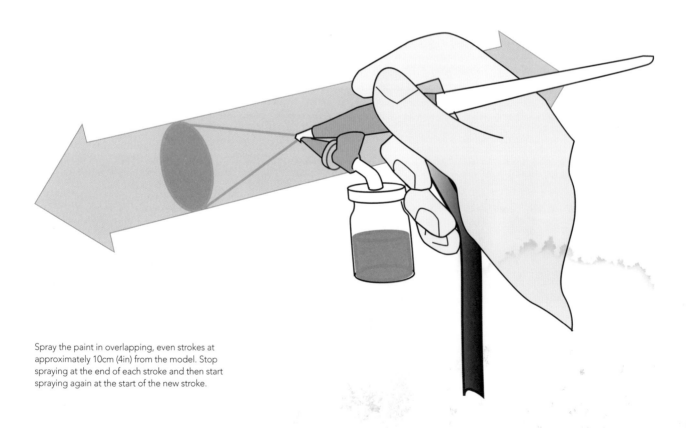

Spray the paint in overlapping, even strokes at approximately 10cm (4in) from the model. Stop spraying at the end of each stroke and then start spraying again at the start of the new stroke.

Tutorial   # 3D Printer Part

In this tutorial, a part printed on a Dimension 1200 3D printer (see Chapter 9, page 83) was first finished and then painted. The staircasing seen on 3D printed parts is a result of the process and needs to be filled before painting.

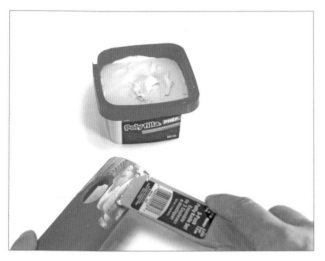

Step 1 The part is first filled with polyfilla and then sanded smooth (see Chapter 9, page 83). If the part does not feel smooth to the touch, repeat the process.

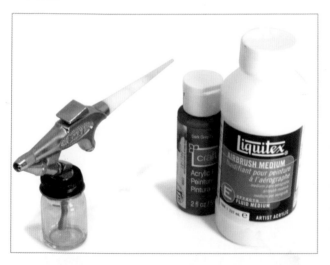

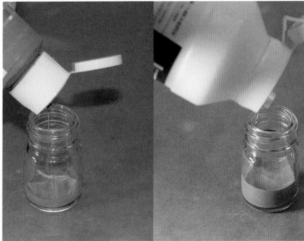

Step 2 A single-action airbrush will be used. An acrylic water-based primer is mixed with approximately 25% water-based airbrush medium as a starting point. A dark-grey primer is chosen for contrast with the filler.

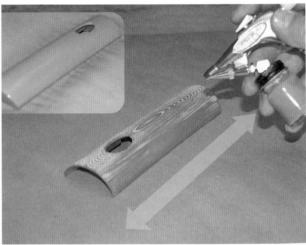

Step 3 The airbrush is now hooked up to the compressor (20–40 PSI) and tested on a scrap piece of plastic in the spray booth. The nozzle flow is adjusted and if the paint is not flowing, more airbrush medium will be added.

The part is then primed in thin layers, which are allowed to dry to the touch between coats. The airbrush is moved back and forth over the part while spraying, but the trigger is released at the end of each stroke and then activated again at the beginning of the new stroke.

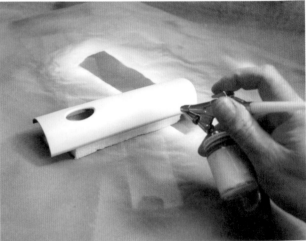

Step 4 Remember that to get a perfect finish, the preparation needs to be perfect. This means that small blemishes and areas missed during the initial filling still need to be touched up. The part is then re-primed and then sanded slightly with 600-grit sandpaper to smooth the primer.

Step 5 With the part primed, the process is repeated with the final paint coat. White semi-gloss water-based acrylic is applied in thin coats. Note how the part is mounted on a piece of Styrofoam to gain access to the lower edges.

GRAPHICS: LABELS AND DECALS

Graphics are used on both low- and high-fidelity models. They are an important aspect of user testing with interactive products. Screens and buttons are labelled so as to test various scenarios of use as well as to communicate functional features. Logos can also add a final touch of realism to models.

The simplest approach is to use the inkjet printer and plain paper to print out a label or graphic. This is certainly acceptable for low-fidelity prototyping. A vector-based illustration program (Adobe Illustrator® or CorelDRAW®) is perfect for laying out the artwork. For low-fidelity prototyping this may be simple line work (see tutorial, page 163), while for higher-fidelity prototyping the artwork can be more advanced with rendered colour and shade. Electronic products with interactive displays typically progress from simple paper prototyping to more realistic appearance models and working prototypes. In order to create an appearance model for an LCD screen it is common to place a printed label behind a piece of clear acrylic. This simulates the depth of the screen.

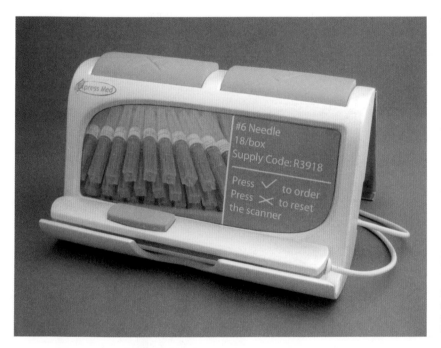

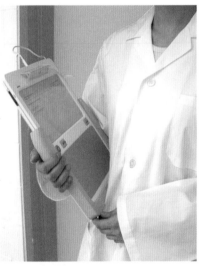

In both of these student projects for healthcare scanners, graphics and labels were an important aspect of both user testing and verifying functionality.

For product logos and other artwork, there are some alternative approaches. Silk-screening is a high-production-quality process, but is expensive. Self-adhesive labels are usually made from vinyl sheet graphics. Vinyl graphic film is sold in numerous colours and finishes and can either be cut by hand or with a digital cutting machine that cuts the outline from a vector file. Printer/cutters are also available that will both print and cut custom artwork on transferable film in practically any colour and finish. They are also available in simulated material finishes such as polished aluminium or carbon fibre. This service can be outsourced to companies that specialize in creating custom signs (available in most cities).

Vinyl films can be used to create high-quality logos. The vinyl is backed with an adhesive.

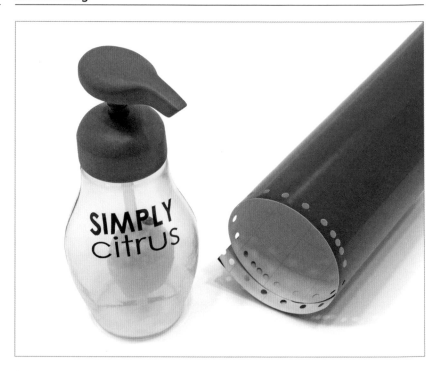

Graphics can be printed on to decal film and transferred to a model. Graphic design tape is also ideal for quickly marking parting lines on low-fidelity models.

Another simple do-it-yourself approach is to use water-transferable decals for modelmaking. These can be custom-printed using a laser printer, cropped and transferred to the model.

Graphic design tape can be used to simulate parting lines. Alternatively decal tapes can be used. See the resources section at the end of the book for suggested suppliers.

Tutorial

Walkie-Talkie

The following tutorial shows how to make a computer-generated layout of the walkie-talkie featured in the XPS foam tutorial (see page 109). This layout is useful for controlling the form of the explorative XPS foam model as well as providing a label for visual details and interface elements. Different arrangements of the interface elements can be created to test various iterations.

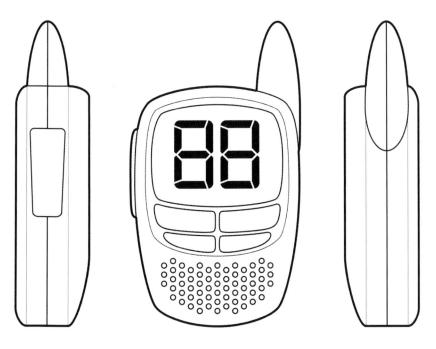

Overview The full-scale 2D rendering layout made in Adobe Illustrator® consists of a front view and two side elevation views.

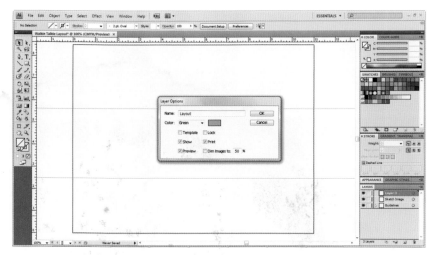

Step 1 The size and orientation is set as desired (e.g. 21.6x28cm/8.5x11in, landscape). Two horizontal guidelines are added, representing the height of the walkie-talkie, by clicking and holding the top ruler bar and dragging to the desired location on the art board. Appropriate layers are then created (e.g. guidelines, sketch image and layout).

Step 2 With the appropriate layer selected, a scanned sketch image is imported, to be used as a template for the layout. The image is scaled to fit accordingly with the guidelines for the height of the walkie-talkie.

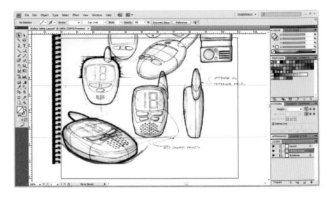

Step 3 With the image selected, reduce the image transparency/opacity (e.g. 40%). With the guidelines layer selected, add a vertical guideline to represent the centre line, which allows for a symmetrical geometry to be traced later on.

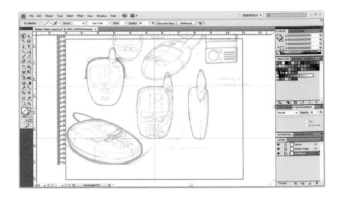

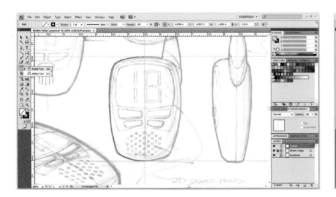

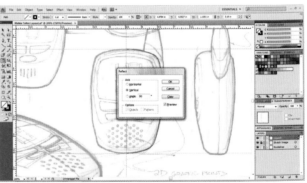

Main Body Step 1 With the layout layer selected, the main body outline is traced using the Pen tool on one side of the centre line.

The second half is created by using a method of copying (the Reflect tool) in which the path of the first half is selected and copied, or reflected, across the vertical centre line. The two paths are then merged together using the Pathfinder tool. This step is repeated to create other elements (e.g. screen and buttons).

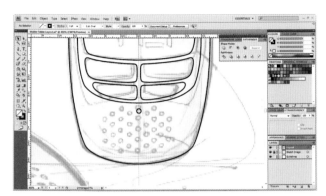

Details Step 1 To create holes for the speaker/microphone, use the Circle or Ellipse tool. First make a small circle centred on the centre guideline.

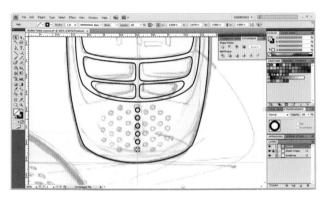

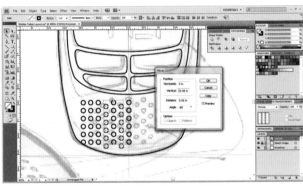

Details Step 2 Make more copies at the same distance in the same direction by selecting a function such as Transform Again as many times as desired.

Repeat the previous step with a Move/Copy in the horizontal direction with the same distance between the points.

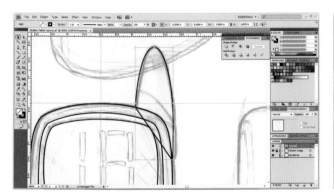

Details Step 3 The antenna is then drawn using the same methods as previously used. It is good practice to close the paths (at least in Illustrator®).

Select the antenna path and trim it against the outer main body path by using a toolset such as Pathfinder. In Illustrator®, this is done by making a copy of the outer body path, pasting it in place (Ctrl F), selecting both the copied outer body path and the antenna path and using either the Minus Back function or the Minus Front function.

Details Step 4 The numbers are added on the screen interface. This can be done by using a font type or by illustrating them. By using the lines of the other elements on the front layout, create more guidelines in order to make the side view.

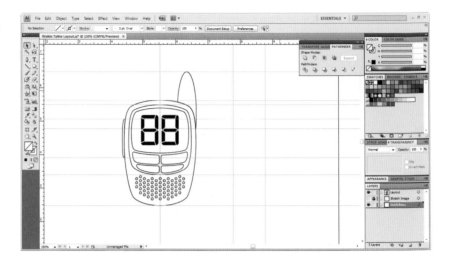

Side View Step 1 A side-profile view is created using the projected guidelines and the previously used tracing methods. Once one side-profile view has been completed, a copy can be reflected across the centre guideline and the elements adjusted appropriately.

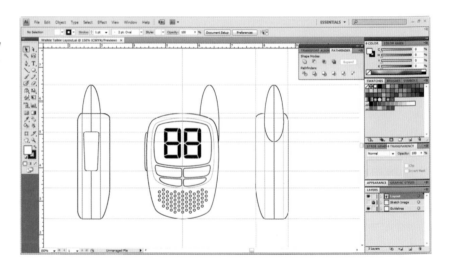

Final Layout Line weights can be adjusted to give a desired visual effect. At this point, the layout is finished. Save your work and print it out for use as a template and/or a label for modelling.

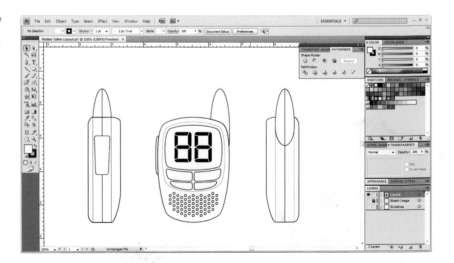

SOFT GOODS: SEWN TEXTILE PRODUCTS

Catherine Brown, Helene Fraser and Louise St. Pierre

Safety Check

— Read Chapter 5 on health and safety
— Obtain professional training and supervision before using your chosen sewing machine

Luggage, backpacks and tents have been around for centuries. Sewn textile products also include safety gear, medical devices, upholstered products, scuba gear, toys and a large array of awning applications. In fact, it is possible to find a sewn product in just about every product-design niche area.

Certain details and material choices are unique to this area of industry. For example:

— Textiles are inherently flexible and can be used in many situations where a product needs to expand, fold, collapse or hinge.
— Textiles can be laminated to one another, or to hard materials, providing complex and specific product qualities (for example, saddles and shoes).
— Textiles can have excellent strength-to-weight ratios (for example, ropes, tents and banners).

Woven calico prototyping fabric.

By handling and discovering textiles and different working techniques one can learn about process and how to be fully in control of the final design.

Textiles fall into two main categories: natural and synthetic. Natural fabrics include cotton, silk, linen and wool, and to the extent that it can be considered a fabric, leather. Synthetic textiles include nylon, polyester and elastane to name a few. In terms of method of manufacture, both natural and synthetic fabrics are generally woven, knitted or felted.

Woven fabrics do not typically have much stretch in the horizontal and vertical direction (although they can be manufactured to do so). These tend to be stiffer and stronger materials.

Knit fabrics come in a variety of weights and constructions (interlock, double knit, jersey, etc.). Their construction allows them much more stretch than a woven fabric, although they are less durable. These fabrics are typically softer against the skin than woven fabric.

Knit with varying textural qualities on the front and back of the fabric.

Felt fabrics are made up of fibres that are matted and pressed together. Felt fabrics are unique in that they have no stretch or grain, but can be moulded when softened with water.

Felts come in varying thickness: the felt on the left is used to create structure internally, while that on the right is more pliable and has many of the qualities of woven fabric.

The textiles used in product design are often more specialized and heavy-duty than those found in the local fabric shop. In addition to the tactile qualities of the material, such issues as UV resistance, tear resistance, heat retention, waterproof capacity, breathability, bonding properties, strength and abrasion resistance have to be taken into consideration. The types of textile appropriate for product design are usually sourced from specialty suppliers, which can also be found on the internet.

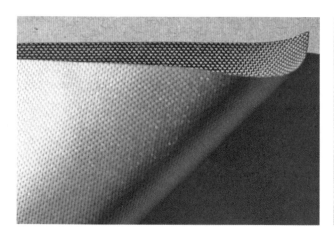

Woven fabric with waterproof backing.

Dyneema® and Spectra® are very high-strength fibres. The image at right shows ripstop fabric with Dyneema® thread in white.

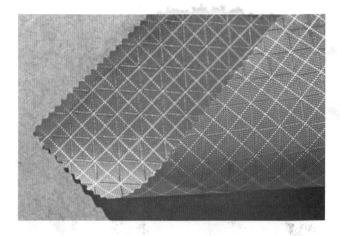

Leather is not strictly a textile, but is used for a variety of products, usually together with fabrics. Leather is both durable and wear-resistant. Some leathers can be sewn with regular sewing machines, although require a special needle. Pigskin and lambskin are softer and easier to sew. Leather-sewing machines are more suitable for leather manufacturing and will handle thicker cowhide. There is a variety of leather types and it is worth finding a good leather retailer to examine and select hides for a project.

Working with Textiles

Initial sketching and form explorations go hand in hand with questions relating to the context of use: is the product meant for water sports, a desert or a winter environment? Is it to be worn, carried or sat on? Suppliers have recommendations and their own application suggestions, but samples should always be obtained and evaluated during the exploration phase of the project.

Hand sketching and vector-based art programs can be used to create side-view renderings, since the complexity of textile form can be hard to model in 3D CAD programs.

Leathers are available in different thicknesses and types.

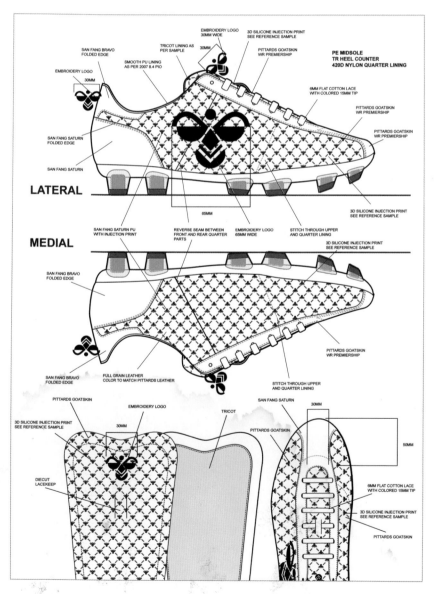

This football shoe layout by Richard Kuchinsky for Hummel was done in Illustrator® and clearly communicates all design details. This could be forwarded with material samples to subcontracted manufacturers for a very detailed prototype. This example also illustrates how soft goods incorporate hardware and custom-moulded parts, such as shoe soles.

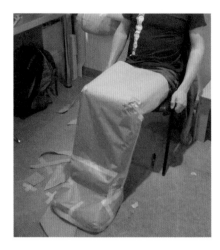

A prototype for a rain-protection garment for wheelchair users is tried out first in paper.

Exploration usually starts in easier-to-work-with materials such as paper and cardboard. Paper is pliable and mimics the behaviour of textile, although it does not droop or sag. It can be used to quickly establish fit and dimension.

Cardboard can be taped or lightly glued together to explore volume and shape (such as for a backpack or purse). The rigidity of these lightweight materials also allows experimenting with seam lines (drawing them on in pencil and then erasing and moving them) and checking whether there is sufficient clearance between features such as multiple pockets and pieces of webbing.

Once the initial form and concept has been established it is advisable to use textiles for further prototypes. Less expensive fabrics such as unbleached calico should be used initially, allowing a number of iterations before moving to the finished product.

 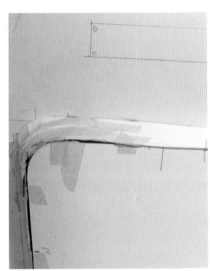

Cardboard is used to establish fit and dimensions for a laptop bag. Details on paper models are pencilled in.

User testing can often be accomplished by modifying existing products. A custom backpack might, for example, be tested initially by modifying an existing pack. This approach is often more effective than building something from scratch, especially if it is only a works-like model.

There is a variety of ways in which to attach fabrics together. The following breakdown outlines some of the advantages and disadvantages.

Quick Attachment Methods

Masking tape allows for quick joining of fabric sections. Tape, unlike pins and staples, can give a much closer indication of how forms behave with seams. It also allows the prototype to be cut apart to make a pattern.

Taping is fast and effective.

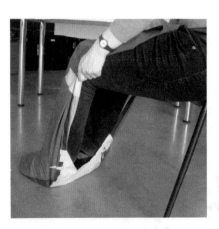 

Pins can be placed parallel or perpendicular to the seam line. It is important to note that pins are best for lighter-weight fabrics and should never be used with any textile that is coated or laminated to be waterproof, as when they are removed they leave holes. The pins are also sharp, which means they pose a mechanical hazard.

Staples can be applied to paper and fabric. Staples will not work for light, soft textiles, but are very effective on stiff fabrics.

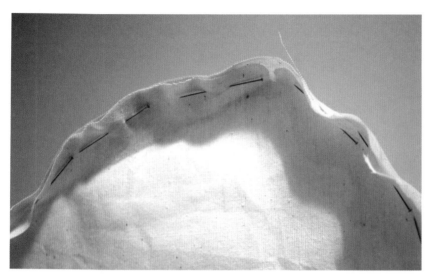

Staples are often used when rapid prototyping with paper, cardboard and fabric. Pins have the advantage of allowing the designer to move directly into a sewing application.

Seams and Allowances

Learning how to sew requires training and practice. It is often a surprise to the uninitiated how difficult it is to achieve a finished look. A prototype may need to be redone a few times in order to get to a satisfactory look. A high-quality finish may require outsourcing the final appearance prototype to a professional. Product designers working in connection with production facilities will have access to highly skilled labour and specialized machinery, where sample-sewing operators work in tandem with the designers to create new prototypes. The sample-sewer's role is to sew and trouble-shoot with the designer in considering construction options to produce high-end product outcomes. Whether doing the sewing by oneself or not, it is useful to understand the basics of sewing.

A product is usually sewn inside out and then turned right-side out to hide the seam allowance and display the aesthetic, finished side.

'Thinking inside out' is necessary, since pieces are usually sewn inside out. The band of fabric between the seam line and the raw edge of the fabric is called a seam allowance. Enclosed seams are ones where the seam allowances will not be exposed to any rubbing, or seen by the user. Stuffed animals and fully lined garments and bags are comprised almost entirely of enclosed seams. Exposed seams are ones whose allowances can be seen and will be exposed to rubbing. These can be found in the interior of backpacks, shoes and unlined clothing. Exposed seams are susceptible to fraying and need to be finished.

There are many different types of seams and finishing options as shown below.

Regular Seams The face sides of two pieces are attached via a straight stitch.

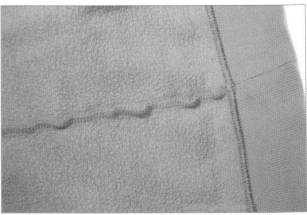

Overlocked Seams These are commonly used for garments constructed out of knit fabric and require a specialized machine called an overlocker. This both sews and finishes the seam simultaneously – in which case it allows the seam a degree of stretch complementary to the fabric – or can be used after a regular seam simply to finish the raw edge.

Flat-Fell or Lap Seams This type of seam is constructed by overlapping one seam allowance over the other. This seam is used in jeans, sportswear and underwear, as it is comfortable for the wearer.

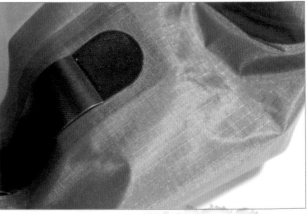

Glued Seams Certain seams are glued in order to replicate more advanced production techniques such as RF (radio frequency) welding or heat bonding. RF-welded seams are most common where a product must be completely airtight or watertight. One can imitate the effect by overlapping and gluing weldable fabrics together, such as neoprene.

Patterns

A pattern is a template that is traced on to textiles. In some cases it is possible to reverse-engineer existing products by taking them apart and then using them as a basis for a new pattern. However, when a unique and new product has been envisioned as a paper prototype, it can also easily be converted into a pattern. This would start by marking all the seam lines on the paper prototype and then cutting it apart. Before cutting the curved seams, marks are drawn perpendicular to the seam line that can be seen clearly on both pieces of fabric. These will be used to create notches that aid in matching sides of a seam together correctly and with ease. The process is clearly illustrated in the kite-surfing glove case study on pages 177–179.

With the prototype cut apart and flattened, seam allowances need to be added to all the pieces. This is done by copying the outline to a new piece of paper and offsetting the seam with a see-through ruler or by manual measurement. The new pattern piece is then cut and notches are added for matching different parts.

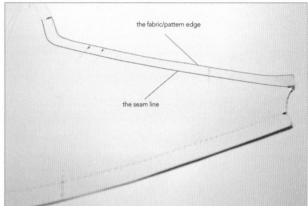

the fabric/pattern edge

the seam line

The patterns are labelled so that it is clear which pieces go where. The grain line runs parallel to the selvedge (self-finished edge) of fabrics. With woven fabrics the yarns running in this direction offer the least amount of stretch and consequently resist bagging and stretching. For this reason, the grain line is identified on all pattern pieces, by marking a line the entire length of the piece. The visible outside should also be marked 'right side up', so that the piece is transferred correctly. Finally, it should be noted that the first pattern is not final. By the time the first prototype is made, it is expected that some changes will happen. This is, in other words, an iterative process, just as with hard materials. It is therefore important to keep the patterns so that they can be modified to add or subtract a bit of material as needed.

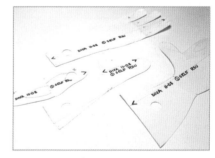

Marked pattern pieces showing name, right side up and grain line.

Be sure to weigh each pattern piece down at either end.

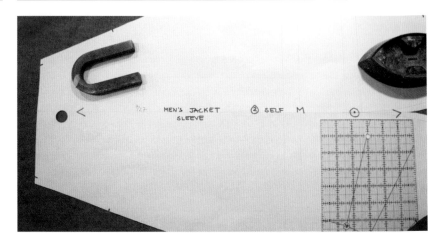

The next step is to mark the pattern on to the fabric. In order to ensure that the pattern pieces do not shift out of position it is advisable to weigh each pattern piece down at either end. If the fabric has stretch qualities, or a visible nap (like corduroy), the tops of all of pattern pieces are aligned in the same direction. A pencil or wax marker is then used to trace the outline, including the notches.

Three-Dimensional Manipulation of Fabric

Three-dimensional forms can be created out of cloth, using its inherent qualities that allow it to be folded and bent into shape. Darts pinch together portions of fabric, while, conversely, gathers and tolerance (ease) work to create volume by forcing additional fabric into a designated area. Widely used in garment construction, these techniques allow fabric to flow smoothly over and around the human torso, but can also be seen in footwear, backpacks and bags. Both tolerance and gathers use the same method, the difference being in the ratio of fabric they manipulate. Pleats and tucks are a way of making a section of cloth narrower in width. Pleats can be found in garments, upholstery, backpacks and bags, as well as in architectural applications.

Darts pinch out a triangular section of cloth to create form.

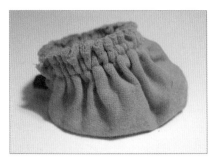

Gathering is a method of pulling fabric in to fit a smaller area, creating intentional puckering.

Tolerance pulls fabric in to fit a smaller area without causing any puckers.

Pleats are folds created by doubling the fabric back on itself and securing at either one end or in multiple places.

Lamination and Layering for Reinforcement and Performance

In order to strengthen cloth in critical areas it usually needs some type of reinforcement. Other materials, such as foam and even formed plastic shapes or cardboard, can be inserted as necessary. It is helpful to examine existing products and study how they are made for inspiration. Custom-made inserts can be formed from plastic (see Chapter 13, page 114) or even cast in silicone (see Chapter 17, page 147), and sewn directly on to the fabric as long as the design and the sewing machine allow for it. Another common use for lamination is to combine performance characteristics. Shell waterproof jackets consist of a waterproof breathable layer laminated to a face fabric. A similar thing is done to make bag fabrics waterproof, with a polyurethane coating being applied to the back of the fabric. It is also common to laminate a more robust outer layer to a soft inner layer for comfort and/or warmth (think of a fleece-lined boot).

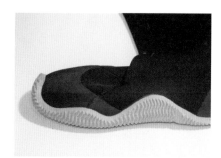

Where performance is needed, other materials can be laminated to the fabric, such as the sole for this boot.

Textile Hardware

Familiar fasteners include buttons, zips, hook and loop tape (Velcro®), snaps and buckles. Specialty textile hardware suppliers have more options than what is typically found in fabric shops.

Buttons and Snaps

Buttons are sewn on and need a buttonhole on the matching fabric. The buttonhole is a slot that has been finished with a sewn edge so that it provides strength and does not unravel. Modern sewing machines have automatic buttonhole features. Snaps, on the other hand, require special snap tools. The tougher snaps should be the type that is riveted in place, using a special rivet tool.

Zips

There is a wide variety of zips available, including metal as well as plastic or waterproof zips. The strength of the zip is often a function of size, and rugged zips may need to be ordered from online sources. Closed zips, where the zip is closed at both ends, are often found on bags.

Snaps need to be riveted in place and consist of four parts.

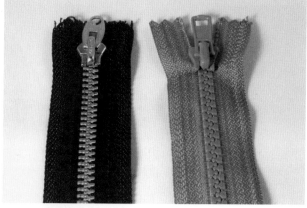

Zips are available in plastic and metal and come in many different colours and sizes.

Velcro® comes in many different widths.

Plastic buckles have many applications and are used with straps.

Elastic cords are available as flat strap or round cord.

Bias binding is used to finish exposed fabric edges so they do not fray.

Hook and Loop Tape

Hook and loop (Velcro®) tape is sewn directly on to fabric and is a versatile material available in a range of colours and widths as well as materials.

Snap-Fit Buckles and Straps

Straps and cords are frequently used on textile products for handles and to add strength. They are used in conjunction with plastic buckles in a number of ways. Strapping is available in a range of materials (usually polypropylene or nylon) and colours. The snap-fit buckles are also available in a wide variety of sizes and shapes. There are also round cords that may be more suitable than the flat strap, depending on the application.

Elastic Cord and Strapping

Elastic materials have a lot of stretch and tend to be used for their clamping strength, for example, the bungee cord. Elastic straps are also used to secure items such as bottles inside a bag.

Bias Binding

Bias binding, or binding tape, serves to sandwich the seam allowance and is sewn on after a regular seam is constructed but before any topstitching is done. It can be applied along external or internal seams.

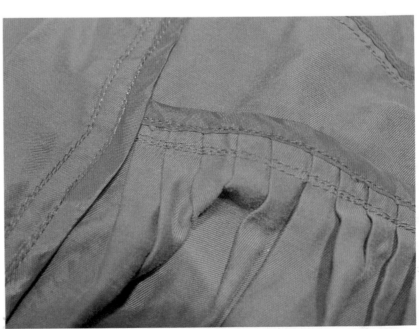

Case Study Kite-Surfing Glove

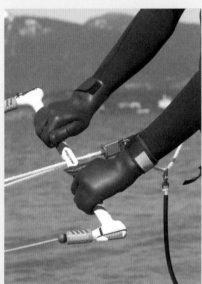

The kite-surfing glove has to provide insulation and is specially designed for gripping the support bar.

The frigid waters off Vancouver and North America's Pacific Coast in general necessitate the use of a wetsuit to insulate against the cold in watersports. These kite-surfing gloves, designed by David Westwood (Emily Carr University, Vancouver) keep the user's hands warm and have been specifically tailored to allow holding the round control bar without creating fatigue in the forearms. The material selection for the gloves is therefore a primary concern, since the material has to be suitably warm while providing the right grip and comfort. The final design is made from a 3mm-thick neoprene incorporating a thin exterior sealed skin layer and is kept secure with an adjustable Velcro® strap.

The form of the kite-surfing glove first had to be modelled on to the human hand, as the shape is unique, incorporating pre-bent fingers (180 degrees) to allow the user to grip an object without having to work against the glove. Typical gloves are designed to be open, but with neoprene gloves this causes fatigue in the hands in only a few minutes, since the wearer is working against the material.

Whereas several iterations were necessary in order to work out the details of fit and function, the workflow for creating the patterns was essentially the same. This involved defining the seam lines by drawing them directly on to the paper model. Marks were then drawn perpendicular to any curved seam line, in order to create notches to aid in matching sides of a seam together correctly and with tolerance. The next step was to disassemble the model by cutting it apart on the seam lines. These pieces were traced to a new piece of paper, at which stage the design could be tweaked. Seam allowances were also added at this stage, along with notches that help in aligning the various pieces. This new pattern could be used to transfer the design to a new prototype.

The form was further developed through several iterations that were conducted in conjunction with user testing. The form progressed in the same fashion, by adding and subtracting material where needed and creating new patterns. The palm of the glove is synthetic leather incorporated both for its durability and its tactility. Neoprene dulls the feedback the user gets through the gloves and will lead to over-gripping of an object. In the course of even a few minutes this over-gripping leads to fatigue. The seams were also glued and trimmed in order to replicate the bonded type of seam construction.

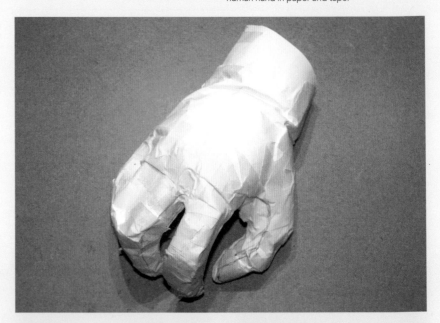

The initial form is modelled directly on to the human hand in paper and tape.

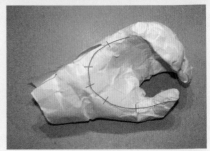

Lines are marked on the glove to define seams (above left). Perpendicular notch lines are also added so as to help with alignment between the different pieces (above right).

The paper prototype is cut apart along the seam lines. These pieces were traced on new paper, adding seam allowances and notches. This was the first set of patterns (above right) and was now ready to be transferred to neoprene.

A mid-stage prototype with corrections marked in pen.

Design for the second (far left) and fourth (left) iterations are captured on paper patterns.

A sewn neoprene prototype is shown left. The seam lines are glued with a rubber sealant and trimmed short to replicate a bonded seam construction.

Glossary

3D printer A category of rapid prototyping machines suitable for office environments that can be networked and used with little training. Rapid prototyping machines build physical three-dimensional parts for CAD files, layer by layer, using a variety of materials and processes.

A

ABS (Acrylonitrile Butadiene Styrene) A common injection-mouldable plastic found in many consumer products including appliances, toys and electronics. It has good strength, processability and cost.

acrylic Clear transparent plastic material, sold in various sheet thicknesses as well as in extruded or cast shapes.

airbrush Used for spray painting. There are two kinds of airbrushes. The simplest is the single-action airbrush, which only has control of the amount of air going through the nozzle. A dual-action airbrush mixes the paint internally and can control both the airflow and the amount of paint.

analogue Without digital input – such as when made by hand or with non-digital tools.

analyze In CAD, analytical tools are used to better visualize the shape and form, or to understand the product's behaviour under load.

appearance prototype Examines the visual aspects of the design and may possibly be used to evaluate user interaction.

armature In modelmaking, an interior structure that provides support for the model. Large clay models are built on armatures of wood or polystyrene foam, which also reduce the amount of clay needed.

artefact An object created by humans.

automobile body filler A two-part resin filler that is used to repair sheet metal dents in automobiles. Polyester is the more common type of resin used.

B

bandsaw A stationary power tool that has a continuous blade that spins in a continuous circular motion. The teeth on the saw blade pull the material of the workpiece down towards a stationary table. Bandsaws can cut intricate shapes and material is fed through the blade.

blow moulding A manufacturing process that is used to produce hollow plastic parts such as plastic bottles and many toys. It starts by inserting an unshaped mass of plastic (a parison) into a hollow metal mould, which is then expanded with compressed air until it contacts the walls of the mould.

breadboard A low-fidelity works-like prototype. It can either be an electronic breadboard or an early explorative mechanical prototype.

C

CAD (Computer Aided Design) Computer application programs for creating models and drawings. Older applications were essentially 2D drafting programs, giving way to more advanced 3D applications that support surface and/or solid object creation. The digital models can be used to create 2D drawings as well as output directly to digital prototyping technologies such as CNC machining and 3D printing.

caliper(s) A precision measurement tool that is used to measure the distance between two opposing sides on a part. Digital readouts allow the measurement to be recorded.

cavity In casting, the cavity is the main part of the mould that defines the outside of the part as opposed to the core that defines the inside of the part. Open moulds only have a cavity and no core.

chipboard An engineered wood product sold in sheets. It is made from wood shavings that have been compressed with heat and glue to create a sheet material. Chipboard has a rough texture and is often laminated with a surface film or thin veneer to improve appearance.

chuck A mounting device for attaching cutting tools to a drilling machine. They are also used to mount a piece of stock in a lathe.

clean-up In modelmaking, clean-up includes cleaning tools and workbenches and the work area.

CNC (Computer Numerical Control) Computer Numerical Control refers to a computer-controlled machine, for example a computer-controlled mill.

collet A special type of chuck for mounting tools or workpiece in a lathe or milling machine.

comprehensive project A project of a larger scope and consisting of different phases of development including exploration, testing and verification.

compressor A machine that compresses air into a tank or through a hose, so that it can be used to drive an airbrush or spray-paint gun.

conceptualization The idea-generating phase of a project utilizing sketches and simple models to help explore and visualize ideas.

configuration An early prototype that looks at how parts or elements of the product will be arranged.

context of use An examination of the product's function and purpose in its intended envrionment and by its intended end users.

core In casting, the core is the part of a two-sided mould that creates the inside of the part.

CorelDRAW® A software illustration package made by Corel Corporation.

cyanoacrylates Fast acting glues also known as super or instant glues.

D

decal In modelmaking, a custom-printed graphic label using a thin film that can be transferred onto the model. It is useful to simulate various graphic printing techniques such as silk-screening.

die-cast A process of casting metal objects by pouring the molten metal into a die – a non-ferrous metal mould.

digital Digital prototyping both refers to the creation of data on the computer as well as digital output from printers.

dowel(s) A round rod of material, usually wood.

drafting tape Low-tack tape that also is less likely to damage paint and paper.

drill speed chart A chart that shows the recommended drill speed based on drill diameter and the material being drilled.

durometer A measure of hardness for plastic and rubber. It is measured on the Shore A (rubber) or Shore D (plastic) units. A bicycle inner tube has an approximate reading of 50 Shore A on the durometer scale.

dust mask Personal protective equipment worn over the nose and mouth that helps filter airborne dust.

dust-collection system Engineering control that removes dust from the environment. It is usually attached to power equipment so that dust is vacuumed into a collector.

E

elastane A high-stretch textile (better known by its trade name lycra) often used in clothing where a tight fit is required, such as with bras, swimwear and bicycle shorts.

elastomer An elastic plastic material that has the same flexible and soft properties as natural rubber, and is available in a range of specific durometer readings.

end mill The standard cutting tool for the milling machine, available in two- or four-flute designs. End mills come in different diameters and lengths, and are suitable to a variety of cutting operations.

end user A term referring to the intended user of the product.

end-grain The end of a piece of wood. The grain runs along the vertical axis of the tree, so the end-grain is visible where the fibres have been cut along the length of the wood.

engineering controls In modelmaking, engineering controls are installed to provide protective measures such as the removal of dust and paint particles through a dust collection system and spray booth.

epoxy A two-part glue, putty or filler that tends to have strong adhesive properties.

ergonomic A comfortable and usable form or fit that reduces strain and stress on the human body.

F

fabrication A manufacturing process that consists of cutting and creating pieces that are then joined together. Metal fabrication involves welding or mechanical fastening using screws and bolts or rivets.

faceplate A disc onto which a workpiece can be affixed when using a lathe.

FDM (fused deposition modelling) A rapid prototyping process that works by feeding a thin filament of ABS into a heated extrusion head. FDM is available both as high-end industrial machinery or as smaller 3D printer systems.

FEA (finite element analysis) A computer software application that allows stresses and strains to be evaluated on a 3D computer model.

fidelity Level of detail and resolution in a prototype.

finishing This includes the final operations of sanding, priming and painting.

fixturing A way of providing an attachment while working, often using clamps or mechanical means.

flash Material that seeps out on the mould parting line as a result of pressure or a loose fit.

foam A material that has been expanded through gassing during the manufacturing process, thereby lowering the density.

foamboard A sheet material consisting of a polystyrene foam sheet laminated between two layers of smooth paper, and producing a lightweight yet rigid structure.

fume hood A ventilation device that is used to draw noxious fumes or dust away from the work. There are many different types and styles available; they should be properly engineered for the particular work at hand so as to minimize any exposure.

functional prototype Examines a functional aspect of the product but does not attempt to look like the real product. Also see works-like prototype.

H

hand saw Hand-held saws vary in size and function. Small-sized and small-toothed hand saws are used in modelmaking to cut plastic and polyurethane foam.

handforming Working and making by hand.

hardboard A thin, compressed board made from wood fibres, also sold as Masonite.

hazard An immediate or long-term danger that can either be mechanical or chemical.

heat gun Hand-held tool that is used to heatform plastic. It looks like a hair dryer but produces much more heat.

hot glue A solid, usually circular glue stick that is applied with a hot glue gun.

I

Illustrator® A vector-based graphic design drawing program by Adobe Corporation.

in-house Referring to modelmaking that is done on the premises of the design company. Some materials can be worked at the desktop, whereas others require more elaborate shop environments.

inclusive design A design process that tries to make products usable for a broader group of people, including those with physical and mental impairments, without special adaptation.

infiltration In the context of rapid prototyping this term refers to absorbing a secondary material (usually a liquid) to strengthen the material characteristics of the prototype.

injection moulding A mass-production plastic moulding process using hollow moulds that are injected with molten plastic under high pressure.

interaction Refers to the human interaction with the product and system. In prototyping, the term refers to the method of observing and studying interaction between a person and a prototype as a series of steps or tasks.

interference checking In computer aided design, a software tool that checks if parts fit properly together in a digital assembly.

iteration Repeating a process in order to achieve a better result.

J

jig A set-up that is used to do a repetitive task and to control a dimension.

L

laminate Joining of sheet material to increase thickness or add strength.

laser (light amplification by stimulated emission of radiation) A laser allows light to be concentrated into a very sharp and strong beam.

laser cutting Using a laser to perform a cutting operation.

lathe Machine that rotates a workpiece against a cutting tool thus removing material to create radial symmetry.

layout A planning document that lays out the parts of the product. It can be drawn by hand as a sketch early in the project or in a vector-based graphic design program or in computer-aided design programs.

looks-like prototype A prototype that examines the visual aspects of the design and may possibly be used to evaluate user interaction.

M

machine tool A range of professional tools used to perform machining operations, such as milling and turning on the lathe.

masking tape Used to mask certain areas when painting.

masonite see hardboard.

MDF (medium density fibreboard) An engineered wood product sold in sheets. It is made from fine wood fibres that have been compressed with heat and glue to have a higher density than chipboard. There is no grain in the material and it cuts very clean and paints with very little sealing. The material may include formaldehyde, which has health concerns and can pose a problem for indoor air quality.

mill Machine tool that rotates a cutter (usually an end-mill) against a fixed workpiece to remove material.

mock-up Another term for a low-fidelity, explorative prototype.

modelling board A sheet material specifically developed for modelmaking. The modelling board is made from polyurethane resin and is available in various densities.

modelmaking The act of making a model.

mould A mould is used to cast or inject material that will take the shape of the mould when it sets. One-sided moulds are open at the top and the material is poured in until it fills this cavity. Two-sided moulds are more complicated and require sprues to pour the material into them as well as vents to allow entrapped air to escape from them.

N

neoprene Synthetic rubber material that is usually foamed. Often found in wetsuits and other soft-sewn products.

O

organic solvent Organic solvents are chemical liquids, such as paint thinner. They are used to dissolve oils, glue, plastic and fillers. They can be very toxic.

outsourcing When models are sent to be made at service bureaus that specialize in modelmaking.

P

pattern In casting, the pattern is used as a three-dimensional template for mould creation. Usually silicone is cast around the pattern to make the mould.

personal risk assessment All work should start with a personal assessment of risk. This includes understanding safety aspects and taking the time to read safety data sheets and instruction labels. It also means wearing appropriate clothing and proper protective equipment for the work at hand.

perspex A flexible acrylic sheet material.

photopolymer In rapid prototyping, this is a solution that selectively cures when exposed to light of a certain wavelength.

photorealistic rendering A very realistic rendering of a product or environment utilizing 3D software applications.

plywood A wooden sheet material made by laminating at least three thin sheets of wood veneer at right angles to each other.

PMS (Pantone Matching System®) Standardized colour matching system used to specify and match colour on products and graphics. Includes CMYK specifications as well as chip samples.

polycarbonate Plastic polymer characterized by toughness.

polyfilla A water-based household filler for wall repair.

polymer Chains of molecules strung together to form a material structure. Plastics are a form of polymer.

polypropylene Plastic polymer characterized by good chemical resistance.

polystyrene A thermoplastic material often used in modelmaking and characterized by ease of processing and low cost. Sold either as styrene sheet and extruded shape or as extruded polystyrene foam (XPS) sheet used as insulation.

polyurethane A plastic polymer material that is available as pre-cast modelling board, or in two-part formulations for casting parts in silicone moulds. Polyurethane glues are strong glues catalyzed by water moisture. Polyurethane paints are also available.

power tool Motorized tools such as drills, saws and sanders. Stationary power tools are installed in a shop space whereas hand-held tools are portable.

pre-production prototype A prototype that closely resembles all aspects of the final product apart from being mass produced.

R

radius gauge A gauge made of thin sheet metal or plastic to measure the inside or outside radius of an edge on the model. They are usually sold in sets, but can also be made easily in styrene.

rapid prototyping An additive computer-controlled process that builds parts inside a machine, layer by layer, using either a powder-, solid- or liquid-based process.

rasp Rasps are hand-held files with large teeth and are essential for rough shaping of wood and other soft materials.

resin In casting, a two-part polymer that sets with rubber-like or hard-plastic properties. Includes silicone and polyurethane resin.

respirator Personal protection equipment worn over the nose and mouth to filter specific particulates and vapours, depending on the specific design of the respirator.

reverse engineering and reverse design In physical prototyping, this involves measuring a handmade model with manual tools or a laser scanner in order to obtain coordinates or surface geometry and input to a computer-aided design program.

Rhino (Rhinoceros®) 3D CAD application program by Robert McNeel & Associates.

roughing operation This involves removal of a large amount of material with a rough tool, such as a rasp, and leaving some material for a finishing operation. When using CNC machines the roughing is usually accomplished with a larger tool and larger step-over so as to remove most of the extra material quickly and effectively.

S

safety glasses Personal protective equipment that protects against sharp or flying objects.

scalpel A popular type of utility knife with a small blade.

SDS (safety data sheets) These contain information on the properties and potential hazards of the material, how to use it safely and what to do if there is an emergency.

sealers In painting, paints that seal the pores of the material before applying colour. These help hide the wood grain or polyurethane pores and create a uniform smooth base for applying paint; useful for higher-fidelity models.

service bureau In prototyping, a business that builds prototypes for a fee. By servicing many different clients they can generate enough cash flow to buy more expensive prototyping machinery. They also have professional modelmakers who specialize in producing high-fidelity prototypes.

set-up In modelmaking, set-up involves the initial fixturing of the workpiece as well as any required safety considerations before a machining operation.

shore scale see durometer.

silica The scientific name for a group of minerals made of silicon and oxygen. Exposure to crystalline silica can cause a number of health problems.

sintering Making a solid object by fusing together a powder substrate. In Selective Laser Sintering (SLS), various substrates are sintered into solid objects through a rapid prototyping process.

SLA (Stereolithography Apparatus) A rapid prototyping process that makes use of a UV laser directed onto the surface of a vat of photopolymer.

SLS (Selective Laser Sintering) Proprietary process of fusing powdered material with heat from a laser.

solid model In computer aided design, a digital model that represents a fully enclosed three-dimensional object. This makes it possible to export the model to an STL file format required for rapid prototyping. It also enables design analysis tools such as FEA to be utilized and simplifies visual rendering of the object as well.

SolidWorks® A 3D CAD application program by Dassault Systèmes SolidWorks Corp.

solvent-based In modelmaking, this typically refers to paints and fillers that are made with organic solvents and therefore require an organic solvent, such as turpentine or lacquer, for clean-up.

spray booth A ventilation device that is used to draw away excess paint while spray painting. There are many different types and styles available. They should be properly engineered for the particular work at hand so as to minimize any exposure.

spray paint A process that uses compressed air to atomize paint particles and produce a fine airborne mist of paint that produces a high-quality paint finish. Spray paint is sold in spray cans or achieved through the use of a spray gun or airbrush.

sprue An opening for pouring material into a mould.

stakeholders In product design, a group of people who have a say in the development and or outcome of the product.

Stanley knife A knife with replaceable blades that is used to cut a variety of materials such as cardboard and thin plastic.

step-over In CNC machining, the distance between parallel lines of machining.

STL Stereolithography file format used in rapid prototyping and 3D printing operations.

storyboard The process of using a series of pictures or drawings to display a sequence of events.

strain In engineering, a measure of how much a material has deformed as a result of an applied force. Strain is calculated as a fractional change in length. A positive value indicates a tensile force whereas a negative value is the result of a compressive force. A plastic sheet that has been stretched from 10cm to 10.1cm has experienced a lengthening of 0.1cm, but the tensile strain is found by dividing this by the original length and is thus equal to 0.01 or 1 per cent.

stress In engineering, a measure of force divided by the surface area. A force applied to a thin cross section of material will thus create a higher stress than the same amount of force applied to a thicker cross section.

strip heater Tool for heat-forming plastic. A thermoplastic sheet is laid on the strip heater, which directs heat in a narrow strip along the length of the material, thereby softening it locally along this line so it can be bent.

styrofoam A trademark name for polystyrene foam made by DOW Chemical Company.

sulphur In modelmaking, sulphur is a natural element that is traditionally added to the clay, but gives it an odour and can interfere with casting compounds such as silicone.

sustainable In modelmaking, a more eco-friendly approach in terms of material utilization and disposal.

T

template Templates are used to guide a cutting operation. They can be as simple as a sheet of paper. They can also be made in thicker or more robust materials for multiple use.

tool path In CNC machining, the computer-controlled path that the end of the cutting tool will take.

tooling In manufacturing, tools are used to mass produce parts for products using processes such as injection-moulding, die-casting and blow moulding. These mass-manufacturing tools are typically made from a hard tool steel and allow molten material to be injected to produce high volumes of identical parts quickly and cost effectively. The tooling also ensures that the parts are identical to each other.

turning A machining operation performed on the lathe. The workpiece is rotated, also known as turned, against a cutting tool that removes material to create radial symmetry – for example bowls or cylindrical and conical shapes.

U

undercut In moulding, a feature that will cause the part to be caught in the mould and create a problem in removal after the material sets. Silicone moulds allow a certain amount of undercut since they are inherently flexible. Rubber silicone parts also allow a certain amount of undercut since they also flex enough possibly to twist out of the mould.

usability In prototyping, this refers to the method of using the prototype to explore and verify the ease of use by people for an envisioned product or service.

V

vector-based Software that uses mathematical equations to represent design elements and is therefore scalable up or down without loss of resolution.

veneer These are very thin sheets of wood sliced from a board and are applied to finish the surfaces of furniture.

vent Air openings in a mould that allow entrapped air to escape so that the mould will fill.

vice A tool that allows parts or workpieces to be mounted so as to remain stable during modelmaking.

viscosity Refers to the thickness of the solution and how easily it flows.

W

water-based In modelmaking, these are glues, fillers and paints that can be cleaned up with water and that can typically be diluted with water.

white glue A common craft glue that works well on paper and is similar to carpenter's glue.

workflow Workflow is a systematic step-by-step process of creation.

workpiece The piece of material that is being worked on.

works-like prototype A Prototype that examines a functional aspect of the product but does not attempt to look like the real product.

Resources

Listed below are further readings and resources, including those for particular sections. Please note that additional readings and resources for health and safety are listed on page 50.

General

Burns, Brian. *People Want Toast Not Toasters: Lessons and Maxims for Design and Designing.* Ottawa: BuschekBooks, 2011.

Buxton, Bill. *Sketching User Experiences: Getting the Design Right and the Right Design.* Toronto: Morgan Kaufman, 2007.

Cagan, Jonathan and Craig M. Vogel. *Creating Breakthrough Products: Innovation from Product Planning to Program Approval.* Upper Saddle River NJ: Prentice Hall, 2002.

Hallgrimsson, Bjarki. 'A Model for Every Purpose: A Study on Traditional Versus Digital Model-making Methods for Industrial Designers'. *IDSA Educational Conference.* Phoenix: IDSA, 2008.

Houde, Stephanie and Charles Hill. 'What Do Prototypes Prototype'. In *Handbook of Human-Computer Interaction,* by Prasad Prabhu, Martin Helander and Thomas K Landauer. New York: Elsevier, 1997, p. 367.

Hudson, Jennifer. *Process: 50 Product Designs from Concept to Manufacture.* London: Laurence King Publishing, 2008.

Jackson, Albert and David Day. *The Modelmaker's Handbook.* New York: Knopf, 1981.

Mills, Criss B. *Designing with Models: A Studio Guide to Making and Using Architectural Design Models.* Hoboken NJ: John Wiley and Sons, Inc., 2005.

Moggridge, Bill. *Designing Interactions.* Cambridge MA: MIT Press, 2007.

Olofsson, Erik and Klara Sjolen. *Design Sketching.* Umeå: KEEOS Design Books, 2005.

Schrage, Michael. *Serious Play: How the World's Best Companies Simulate to Innovate.* Boston: Harvard Business School Press, 2000.

Shimizu, Yoshihara, Takashi Kojima, Masazo Tano and Shinji Matsuda. *Models and Prototypes: Clay, Plaster, Styrofoam, Paper.* Tokyo: Graphic-sha Publishing Co., 1991.

Sennet, Richard. *The Craftsman.* New Haven: Yale University Press, 2009.

Terstiege, Gerrit. *The Making of Design: From the First Model to the Final Product.* Basel: Birkhäuser Architecture, 2009.

Thomke, Stefan H. 'Enlightened Experimentation: The New Imperative for Innovation'. In *Harvard Business Review on Innovation,* Cambridge MA: Harvard Business Press, 2001, pp. 179–205.

Trudeau, Norman. *Professional Modelmaking: A Handbook of Techniques and Materials for Architects and Designers.* New York: Whitney Library of Design, 1995.

Ulrich, K. and S.D. Eppinger. *Product Design and Development.* New York: McGraw-Hill, 2003.

Visocky O'Grady, Jennifer, and Kenneth Visocky O'Grady. *A Designer's Research Manual: Succeed in Design by Knowing Your Clients and What They Really Need.* Beverly MA: Rockport, 2009.

1: Characteristics of Prototyping

Fulton-Suri, Jane. 'Informing Our Intuition: Design Research for Radical Innovation'. *Rotman Magazine,* Winter 2008, pp. 53–57.

Kelley, Tom. *The Art of Innovation: Lessons in Creativity from IDEO, America's Leading Design Firm.* New York: Doubleday, 2001.

2: How Prototypes Are Used

MYTO: a cantilever chair. BASF, KGID, PLANK: Ludwigshafen, Munich, Ora, 2008.

Böhm, Florian ed. *KGID Konstantin Grcic Industrial Design.* London: Phaidon Press Limited, 2005.

Dumas, S. Joseph and Janice C. Redish. *A Practical Guide to Usability Testing.* Revised Edition. Exeter: Intellect Books, 1999.

Pallasmaa, Juhani, ed. *Alvar Aalto: Furniture.* Cambridge MA: MIT Press, 1985.

3: Prototyping Interactive Electronic Products

Arduino: http://www.arduino.cc/

Budd, Jim et al. 'Kurio: A Tangible Interactive Museum Guide'. *IDSA Education Conference.* Miami: IDSA, 2009.

Cronin, Dave. *Industry Trends in Prototyping:* http://www.adobe.com/devnet/fireworks/articles/cooper_prototyping.

Kelly, James Floyd. *Lego Mindstorms NXT-G: Programming Guide.* 2nd edition. New York: Apress, 2010.

5: Health and Safety (also see page 50)

Hughes, Phil and Liz Hughes. *Easy Guide to Health and Safety.* Oxford: Elsevier, 2008.

McCann, Michael P. and Angela Babin. *Health Hazards Manual for Artists.* 6th edition. Guilford CT: Lyons Press, 2008.

Rossol, Manona. *The Artist's Complete Health and Safety Guide.* 3rd edition. New York: Allworth Press, 2001.

7: Workflow

NextEngine's 3D laser scanner: http://www.nextengine.com

Z Corporation's 3D scanners: http://www.zcorp.com

8: Tools

Chua, C.K., K.F. Leong and C.S. Lim. *Rapid Prototyping; Principles and Applications.* Singapore: World Scientific Publishing Co, 2003.

WOOD Magazine's 'Drill Press Speed Chart' http://www.woodmagazine.com/woodworking-tips/techniques/drilling-boring/drill-press-speed-chart/

Grimm, Todd. *User's Guide to Rapid Prototyping.* Dearborn MI: Society of Manufacturing Engineers, 2004.

Walker, John R. *Machining Fundamentals.* vol. 8. Tinley Park IL: Goodheart-Wilcox, 2004.

9: Adhesives and Fillers

Woodsmith magazine's 'Glue Application Chart' http://www.woodsmith.com/magazine/extras/134/glue-application-chart/

Aves' Apoxie® Sculpt: http://www.avesstudio.com.

Flash Glue: http://www.flashglue.com

Zap Glue: http://www.zapglue.com

10: Paper

Jackson, Paul. *Folding Techniques for Designers: From Sheet to Form.* London: Laurence King Publishing, 2011.

13: Thermoplastic Sheet and Extruded Shapes

De Leeuw, Martien. *Series and Mass Production Technology for Product Design.* Ottawa: School of Industrial Design, Carleton University.

Evergreen Scale Models' plastic shapes: http://www.evergreenscalemodels.com/Shapes

Muccio, Edward. *Plastic Part Technology.* Materials Park OH: ASM, 1991.

14: Polyurethane Modelling Board

General Plastics' Knowledge Center: http://www.generalplastics.com/knowledge-center

Freeman's Renshape modelling and styling board: http://www.freemansupply.com/RenShapeModelingan.htm

15: Wood

Bird, Lonnie. *The Bandsaw Book.* NewTown CT: Taunton Press, 1999.

Gibbs, Nick, *The Real Wood Bible: The Complete Illustrtated Guide to Choosing and Using 100 Decorative Woods.* Buffalo NY: Firefly Books, 2005.

16: Modelling Clay

Chavant Inc.: http://www.chavant.com

Kolb Technology: http://www.kolb-technology.com

Van Doren, Harold. *Industrial Design: A Practical Guide.* New York: McGraw-Hill, 1940.

17: Casting

Smooth-On Inc's mould-making and casting materials: http://www.smooth-on.com

Alumilite's casting resin and silicone mould-making rubber: http://www.alumilite.com

18: Painting: More than an Afterthought

Liquitex. *The Acrylic Book: A Comprehensive Resource for Artists:* http://wwwliquitex.com/acrylicbook/

Peacock, Ian. *Painting and Finishing Models.* Poole: Special Interest Model Books, 1998.

Wilson, Jeff, Robert Downie, and Jeff Herne. *Airbrushing Basics.* Waukesha Wi: Kalmbach Publishing Co, 2006.

Index

Picture credits

The author and Laurence King Publishing Ltd wish to thank the institutions and individuals who have kindly provided photographic material for use in this book. Sources for illustrations and copyright credits are given below. While every effort has been made to trace the present copyright holders, the publishers and author apologize in advance for any unintentional omission or error, and will be pleased to insert the appropriate acknowledgement in any subsequent edition.

Numbers refer to pages in the book unless otherwise stated.
T = top, B = bottom, L = left, R = right, C = centre

Cover art (front) Courtesy Reebok and Z Corporation, (back) Courtesy Umeå Institute of Design, Umeå University, Umeå, Sweden; 2–3, 86 Courtesy Julien Vallée; 6, 133C Courtesy Fiskars, Daniel J. Lipscomb, Senior Industrial Designer, Fiskars Americas; 7 Courtesy Colin Roberts; 8 Courtesy Fiskars, Daniel J. Lipscomb, Senior Industrial Designer, Fiskars Americas; 9TL Courtesy Wacom; 9BR Courtesy SensAble Technologies, © Copyright SensAble Technologies, Inc.; 11 Courtesy Mixer Design Group: Design Team: Blake West (Mixer Design Group), Lorenzo Dunn (Motion Computing),Brad Vier (Motion Computing), Chris Lenart (Lenart Studios); 12T Courtesy IDEO; 12–13B Courtesy Lunar Design: Project Team: Donna Beals (Manager, Product Development, Oral-B Laboratories), Bill Bredall (Manager, Product Development, Oral-B Laboratories), Bred Castillo (Manager, Product Development, Oral-B Laboratories), Jurgen Greubel (Braun A.G.), Jeff Hoefer (Creative Director, Lunar Imaging Group), Michael Roberts (Manager, The Gillete Company), Jeffrey Salazar (Senior Industrial Designer, Lunar Design), Peter Schneider (Director, Corporate Product Design, Braun A.G.), Maisie Wong-Paredes (Director, Product Development, Oral-B Laboratories), Max Yoshimoto (Vice President, Lunar Design), Other Contributors: Brad Baker (General Manager, Oral-B Laboratories), Diane Cook (Manager, Oral-B Laboratories), Diane Jacobs (Manager, Oral-B Laboratories), Janet Homewood (Director, Oral-B Laboratories), Marie-Anne Low (Manager, Oral-B Laboratories), Craig Masterman (Scientist, Oral-B Laboratories), Jay McCullogh (Manager, Oral-B Laboratories), Tai Ngo (Engineer, Oral-B Laboratories), Diane Rooney (Director, Oral-B Laboratories), David Weber (Director, Oral-B Laboratories); 14 Courtesy Wataru Watanabe; 15–17 Courtesy Vessel Inc., Design: Stefane Barbeau and Duane Smith of Vessel Inc. Manufacturing: OXO International; 18–19 Courtesy Mixer Design Group, Design Team: Blake West (Mixer Design Group), Lorenzo Dunn (Motion Computing), Brad Vier (Motion Computing), Chris Lenart (Lenart Studios); 20T Courtesy 2nd Year Carleton University Students: Theo Stoppels, Mark Fromow, Chuyue Chang, Kevin Spencer, William McDonald, Alyona Iouguina-Yugina, Sisi Tang, Lee Oddy, Yevhen Pityk, Tiziano Cousineau; 20B Courtesy Nike UK. Ltd, www.considereddesign.com; 21T Courtesy Mixer Design Group and Triple Crown Dog Academy, Design Team: Blake West, Bailey Jones, Kristin Will, Jon Anderson; 21B, 26B Courtesy Mixer Design Group and Triple Crown Dog Academy, Design Team: Blake West, Daniel Allert, Julie Heard; 22B, 88BR Courtesy Pollyanna Ling; 24T,

133B Courtesy Arjun Mehta; 24B, 26T Courtesy Insight Product Development and Motorola; 26C Courtesy Headwaters, Design Team: Rudy Vandenbelt, Troy Anderson, Kevin Bailey (Headwaters Research and Development); 27–29, 55, 88CL Courtesy Konstantin Grcic Industrial Design; 30–32, 124B, 126 Courtesy Frog Design, Frog Design Team: Howard Nuk, Brian Cutter, Jonathan Rowell, Remy Labesque, David Gustafson and Ecotality Team: Jonathan Read, Don Karner, Garret Beauregard, Kevin Morrow, Colin Read, Dimitri Hochard, Andy Hooper; 33–34 Courtesy Xoran Technologies, Ann Arbor, MI and Insight Product Development, Chicago, IL; 35–38, 139TR Courtesy NewDeal Design, Design Team: Gadi Amit, Inbal Etgar; 139B Philip Benson, Marvin Lara, Jessica Livingston, Logan Taylor; 39T LEGO® and MINDSTORMS® are trademarks of the LEGO Group of Companies. © 2011 The LEGO Group. All rights reserved; 39B © Silvan Linn 2007–2008. www.silvanlinn.com; 40–41 Courtesy Jim Budd and Ron Wakkary, Design Team: Carleton University (Jim Budd, Bjarki Hallgrimsson, Chad Harber, Colin Roberts, Sherry Radburn-Ong, Ehren Katzur) and Simon Fraser University: (Ron Wakkary, Marek Hatala, Jack Stockholm, Kevin Muise, Karen Tanenbaum, Greg Corness, Bardia Mohabbati); 56T Courtesy NextEngine, NextEngine 3D Scanner, USB 2.0 peripheral with Multi-Stripe Laser Technology (MLT); 56B Courtesy of Z Corporation; 57 © Silvan Linn 2007-2008. www.silvanlinn.com; 63C Turned Vacuum Form by Meghan Marin; 68 Courtesy Jeffrey Burgers; 69T Courtesy 3D Systems Corporation, Selective Laser Sintering SLS Production 3D Printers deliver light weight durable end use parts for applications ranging from aerospace and defence to consumer goods and medical devices; 69C Courtesy Mixer Design Group, Design Team: Blake West (Mixer Design Group), Lorenzo Dunn (Motion Computing),Brad Vier (Motion Computing), Chris Lenart (Lenart Studios); 69B, 70 Courtesy Z Corporation; 71, 72T Courtesy of Stratasys; 72CR Photographs courtesy 3D Systems Corporation: invented in 1986, Stereolithography has revolutionized Product Development. An operator monitors a job in process on an SLA 3D Production Printer; 72BR GasTurbine Laboratory NRC Canada and Synergy Models and Prototypes; 73 © 2010 Objet: Polyjet, Fullcure, Eden 350, Connex, Polyjet Matrix and Digital Materials are trademarks of Objet Geometries and may be registered in certain jurisdictions; 75TR Courtesy Synergy Models and Prototypes, Machined Part: Ciena Systems (Art Van Gaal), Synergy Models and Prototypes (Richard Levesque); 78T Youssef Sayarh; 87B Courtesy Nick Kleemola; 88T Courtesy Tou Yia Thao; 89 Anthony Frank Keeler; 91T Photography Meidad Suchowolski; 96 Courtesy Wai-Loong Lim, founder Y Studios LLC and Sonos Inc.; 105T Courtesy Nancy Mistove Funrise Toys; 105B, 140 Courtesy Umeå Institute of Design, Umeå University, Umeå, Sweden: Olme Spyder was a 10 week-long term project carried out by students attending the MA Programme in Transportation Design at the Umeå Institute of Design, Umeå University, Sweden. Students/authors: Jan Christian Osnes, Travis Vaninetti, Daniel Gunnarsson, Yong-Fei Han, Youngjun Byun, Seyyed Javad Ghaffarian, Eric Leong, Kosin Voravattayagon and Martin Lauritsen; 113T Courtesy Caitie Tzekakis; 113B, 114T Courtesy Dana Douglas, Hallgrimsson Product Development; 115BR

Courtesy Mixer Design Group; 116T Courtesy William Lau, sketches and models for studio project at Carleton University Autumn 2008; 118–119, 133T, 134T Courtesy Michael Defazio; 123 Images courtesy Fuseproject; 132 Courtesy Dennis Cheng; 136B, 137T Courtesy Randy Kerr; 138 Courtesy Alan Okamura; 141, 142 Courtesy Kolb Technology GmbH, Germany, tools photos by Xaver Zistler; 146T Courtesy DW Product Development Inc., Design Team: Mike Sirois, Rob Watters,Romeo Graham, Rodney J. Muir, Colin Roberts, Moulding-Ottawa Mould Craft, Casting Solids Concepts, Inc.; 149B Courtesy Eduardo Mujica; 150 Dark Matters, Simen Leung; 151–153 Courtesy Mark Boycott; 154T Courtesy Colin Roberts; 161 Express Med Scanner Bonnie Van Tassel Fall 2006, NICU Sara Zokaei Fall 2006; 162T Courtesy Paul Chamandy Cook; 169B © Richard Kuchinsky / The Directive Collective, Hummel International A/S; 170T, B Courtesy Sarah Bailey; 177–179 Courtesy David Westwood

Acknowledgements

I would like to thank Kevin Henry of Columbia College for our many inspirational discussions and for introducing me to Laurence King Publishing; Jo Lightfoot, my commissioning editor for seeing the value in a unique and new book on modelmaking, my editors Donald Dinwiddie and Sophie Drysdale for providing helpful, diligent and positive feedback, Kirsty Seymour-Ure for copy-editing, Lisa Cutmore for proofreading and Patrick Morrisey of Unlimited for making the layout so attractive while being challenged with such a wide range of pictures.

I wish to thank all the contributors for their stories and brilliant examples that show how important prototyping is to the problem-solving process. In addition to all the people listed in the picture credits, I also wish to extend a thank you to Chris Cavello of Mixer Design Group, Catie Clark and Arjun Mehta of IDEO, Gerard Furbershaw of Lunar Design, Chad Harber of NewDealDesign and Tara Prasad of Insight Product Development for their help. I also wish to thank Niklas Andersson, Karl Gustav Bergstedt, Johan Gustavson, Demian Horst, and Tomas Lindehell at Umeå Institute of Design, as well as Davide Cuartielles, Simon Niedenthal and Mattias Nordberg at Malmö University for hosting my visits at their institutions in Sweden.

A special thanks to Catherine Brown, Hélène Day-Fraser and Louise St. Pierre for writing Chapter 20 Soft Goods: Sewn Textile Products and Monona Rossol for sharing her insights on health and safety.

My student assistants at Carleton University were wonderful: my thanks to Tim Haats for his extensive help with illustrations and developing the step-by-step tutorials, Shirley Tran for additional pictures and illustrations and Sara Zokai for the energy and enthusiasm she offered during the early parts of the project. And also thanks to our shop technicians Jim Dewar, Terry Flaherty and Walter Zanetti for providing technical support and also for supervising tutorials.

Lastly a project like this takes the support of family and friends: my thanks to David, Andrea and Christa for putting me up during fact-finding trips to San Francisco. And especially thanks to my wife Kim, sons Björn and Kaj and my brother Sigtrygg for being the wonderful people that I love and who have remained enthusiastically supportive.

This book is dedicated to my mother Aranka and father Sigurdur for instilling a love of design and working with my hands, and also never to be ashamed of rolling up my sleeves.